JAZZ MANDOLIN

by TED ESCHLIMAN

Online Audio — www.melbay.com/20835BCDEB

D1706877

Audio Contents

1	FFcP Ionian Mandolin - C	22	Minor World Dominants
2	FFcP Ionian Mandolin - B♭	23	How High the Minor Two
3	FFcP Ionian Mandolin - A♭	24	Maj ii V7 I 2nd
4	FFcP Ionian Mandolin - D	25	Maj ii V7 I 3rd
5	FFcP Move on Up	26	Maj ii V7 I 1st
6	Guides and Gravity	27	Maj ii V7 I 4th
7	Arp Maj7	28	Min ii V7 I 1st
8	Arp Dom7	29	Min ii V7 I 2nd
9	Arp Min7	30	Min ii V7 I 3rd
10	Arp Min6	31	Min ii V7 I 4th
11	Lydian DUDU	32	Chick'n Apple Scrapple
12	Lydia O'Lydia	33	Turnaround 3
13	Dorian Patterns	34	Turnaround 2
14	Dorian's Grey	35	Turnaround 1
15	Berklee Gypsy Drills	36	Turnaround 4
16	Bebop Mandology1	37	Yes, I'll Always Be There
17	Bebop Mandology2	38	Fascinatin' Doll
18	Bebop Mandology3	39	Chick'n Apple Scrapple (Don Stiernberg)
19	Bebop Mandology4	40	Fascinatin' Doll (Don Stiernberg)
20	Minor in Possession	41	Yes, I'll Always Be There (Don Stiernberg)
21	Minor:V7 (♭9) i		

---

1 2 3 4 5 6 7 8 9 0

Visit us on the Web at www.melbay.com — E-mail us at email@melbay.com

Table of Contents

Foreword

It wasn't so long ago that a bootleg copy of an an old Homer & Jethro recording or the work of Tiny Moore with the Bob or Billy Jack Wills bands pretty much summed up the term "jazz mandolin."

No longer. Jazz's influence is a vital part of the today's scene and found in just about every conceivable music genre. Mandolin players are busy venturing into musical territory that 30 years ago, few dared attempt. And while there are a few resources in print, a truly comprehensive jazz mandolin method was waiting to be written. Until now. With Getting Into Jazz Mandolin,

Ted Eschliman has given us the gift of a no-nonsense practical guide to help us incorporate some simple and effective ideas into our musical vocabulary. Let the mystery be no more.

I can't wait to dig into this one.

Scott Tichenor, Site Administrator
www.MandolinCafe.com

Introduction and Philosophy

For the **Bluegrass** or **Folk** mandolinist, the complex harmonic vocabulary of jazz can lure like a siren, yet intimidate like the corner bully. Armed with a little bit of information, some tactile exercises, and an analytically open ear, your wildest dreams of playing jazz will come true!

Jazz doesn't have to be as secret as a fraternity handshake. It doesn't have to be as complex as nuclear physics. The goal of this book is to introduce you to higher level jazz theory, but take you there from a familiar, comfortable starting point: the "**Major Scale**." You'll learn fresh ways to finger it, as well as start it on different notes, but ultimately knowing the inherent half step/whole step relationships of this "folk" material has you down that path already.

We won't smack you with the cerebral, the "*brain*" part of jazz. Let's introduce your **fingers** first. Take time to learn the patterns well. Play them over and over, as calisthenics and as tone development. (If you're serious about learning the mandolin, you'd be doing this anyway!)

The **FFcP** (Four Finger Closed Position) section might be totally foreign to you as your initial dependence on the open strings for reference (*let alone your fear of the pinky finger*) may be as comfortable to you as the womb. This new skill gets you out, past the crib, on to walking, and before long, rock climbing, but you must be willing to give it patience and time.

We'll start by adding new sounds, altering familiar scales slightly. Then we'll learn chord patterns and interact between the two. As this becomes part of your subconscious playing, we'll slap *labels* on them, outlining and categorizing the physical side of playing.

This "autopilot" approach to finger patterns will free your brain to coordinate and create art. With an investment of time, you'll be successfully down the road to improvising and stop in the middle of practicing and say to yourself, "Wow! I don't even know where these notes came from, but they're right there in my fingers!"

Fingers. Ears. Brain. This is the path for this book; this is your outline. Work the exercises committing yourself to clean execution and good tone. Listen to yourself and the sounds coming out of your strings. Then make the labels we present work toward an even larger goal, one of comprehending Jazz and any other music you find yourself involved in. Listen to other good jazz artists and the jazz theory introduced here will make even more sense.

Ted Eschliman,
Author and Perpetual Student of Jazz

Four Finger Closed Position (FFcP)

Introducing the FFcP

Jazz theory is based on relationships. Initially, how chords and scale tones interact, stray, resolve, and move can be overwhelming! We will attempt to debunk the notion that the "mystery" and complexity of jazz can only be unlocked by a privileged few. The virtually infinite combinations within 12 keys can easily be reduced and understood, by adopting the Four Finger Closed Position system (FFcP).

We aren't going to completely drop open strings! But for the purpose of simplifying and reducing the unwieldy amount of options, we're going to build a tactile "home base," to aid in visualizing harmonic function on the fingerboard and "feel" the relationship of common "modes", to the frets.

First, we need to limit the fingerings to just four possibilities. As you study these, understand we are building roadmaps, or better, "wagon trail ruts" of where to intuitively place your fingers during improvisation. Along the way, you'll enjoy the healthy by-product of a useful, limber 4th finger (pinky). And eventually abandon the fear of moving everything up the frets into the fertile potential of the mandolin's higher positions.

We'll also gain skill in identifying which notes are critical in defining tonality and creating tension and resolution.

1st Finger Position:
1st FFcP

Let's look at the first position possibilities. We'll start with the first finger position in the key of A. Note that if you move it down one fret, you come up with the key of A♭. Tone relationships remain intact, as well as fingerings:

Now move it up one string, you have the key of E♭, without learning a new pattern. All your scale degree FUNCTIONS are covered by the same fingers. And if you move this up a fret too, you get the key of E. You now have 4 of the 12 major scales, with only one fingering pattern.

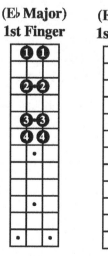

2nd Finger Position:
2nd FFcP

All of the previous scales started with the 1st finger. Now we'll start a Major scale with the 2nd finger, and learn the key of B♭. If you take the same method of shifting, go up a fret, you have B (natural) Major. Up a string, F♯ Major, and back down one Fret, F Major.

3rd Finger Position:
3rd FFcP

We'll designate the 3rd pattern, C Major by starting it with the 3rd finger. Up a fret gives you C♯, up a string would give you the G♯, which is the upper octave of the enharmonic equivalent, A♭. We've already learned that in the 1st position, but now you are set to continue (with little intimidation), up to the second octave. Go back a fret and it's G natural.

4th Finger Position:
4th FFcP

Perhaps a little more foreign but no less significant, would be your final pattern, starting with the pinky. Again, avoid the open string for now; we're discovering relationships in the closed position. Finger the D Major Scale starting with the 4th finger. Move it up a fret, you have an alternate fingering for the E♭ Major you learned previously in the 1st finger position. Same with it's shift up a string, another alternative for A♭, and down, an alternative for A.

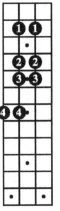

As you get used to the way these feel (and it will be a stretch for that pinky at first!), notice the strength and flexibility you earn with your 4th finger; even your 3rd will become stronger. More importantly, this will allow you to intellectually and with tactile sense, discover important scale degree functions. The "color" defining note of the third degree, the leading tone "pull" of the seventh scale degree-it's all something you want to start to be conscious of, once these fingerings become familiar.

Don't worry about losing out on the open strings for now. Those are easy and they will come right back to you. Work with this system, and don't deny yourself the 25% MORE opportunity a viable pinky can offer your playing!

Half Step Scale Degrees

Most steps in the major scale are two frets apart (a whole step). There are two VERY important exceptions:

> 3rd to 4th scale degrees are one fret (1/2 step)
> 7th to 8th scale degrees are one fret (1/2 step)

These intervals are good to start being aware of, not just because they depart from the other whole step relationships; but also because they are crucial "tension" tones (**Gravity Notes**). The **4th** likes to lead down to the **3rd**, the **7th** likes to lead up to the **8th (1st)**. These help define the tonality when you improvise, the sooner you make this a subconscious awareness, the sooner you can exploit it in your soloing. Try to be conscious of them when you practice the **FFcP** exercises, especially in the "**Guide Tones**" sections toward the end of each exercise.

C = 1	G = 5
D = 2	A = 6
E = 3	B = 7
F = 4	C = 8 *(or 1)*

Review: Principles of FFcP

In this system, there are only four ways to play a major scale: starting with the first finger, the second, the third and the fourth. That's it!

All 12 keys can be covered in only four different positions, simply by transposing up or down the fretboard and across strings.

4th Finger (Pinky) strength and coordination become part of daily development exercises.

Key Chord Tone relationships in improvising become tactile, visible, and intuitively realized.

Position shifts to a second octave are easily bridged merely by starting the next octave with a different FFcP pattern.

Changes in tonal "micro-centers" by half steps easily transition either by moving the pattern by one fret, or using the next FFcP.

IMPORTANT!...

Open string "opportunities" will be explained and added later, but only after mastering the closed FFcP system.

JAZZ MANDOLOGY

Ionian Mandology

Major Scale Studies (Ionian Mode):
Starting on the 3rd Finger

Repeat signs are not arbitrary. Repeat the selections within
these bars as often as you need to make them comfortable. You can't overplay them!

3rd C, C♯, G, A♭
FFcP

Use the "home" pattern (straight major scale) as kind of mental "rest area" so that you can run on "autopilot" and think about what you're doing in the harder sections.

Major Scale Studies (Ionian Mode):
Starting on the 2nd Finger

Now we're going to move everything down two Frets.
It's the same major scale, but we'll start it with the 2nd finger.

2nd Bb, B, F, F#
FFcP

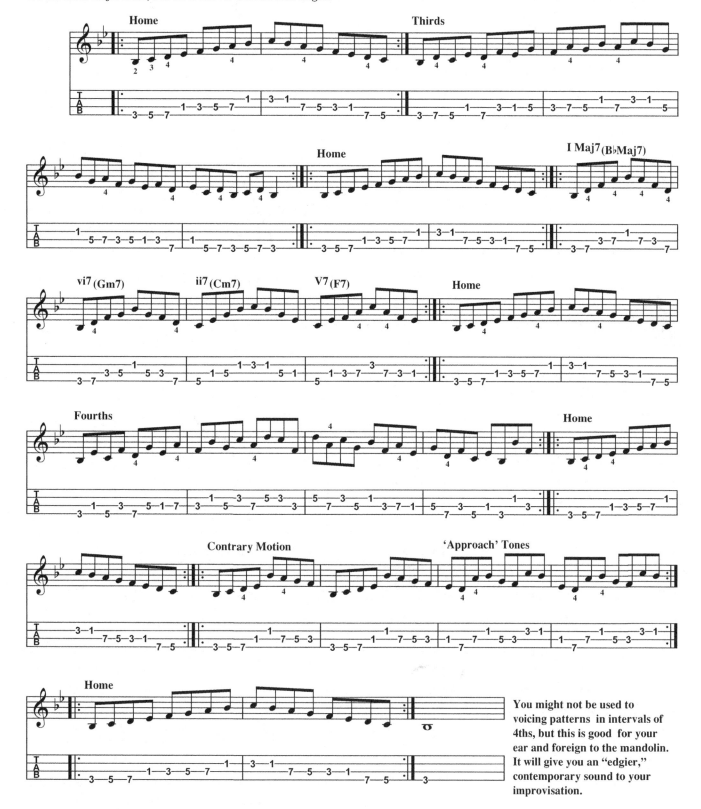

You might not be used to voicing patterns in intervals of 4ths, but this is good for your ear and foreign to the mandolin. It will give you an "edgier," contemporary sound to your improvisation.

Major Scale Studies (Ionian Mode):
Starting on the 1st Finger

1st A♭, A, E♭, E
FFcP

Down two more Frets. Again, same major scale, but we'll start it with the 1st finger.
Note: You'll be using the same fingering for A major, but this gives you more "stretch!!"

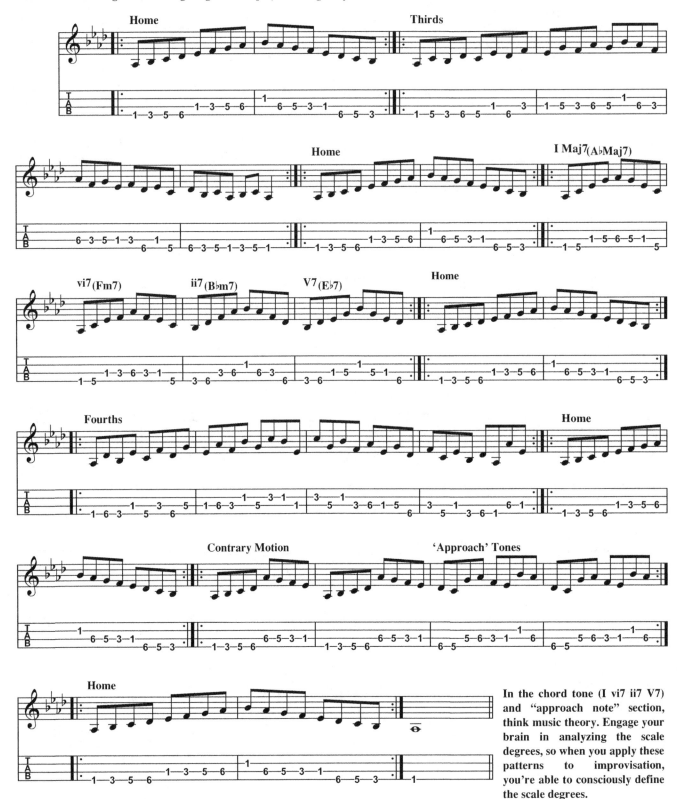

In the chord tone (I vi7 ii7 V7) and "approach note" section, think music theory. Engage your brain in analyzing the scale degrees, so when you apply these patterns to improvisation, you're able to consciously define the scale degrees.

Major Scale Studies (Ionian Mode):
Starting on the 4th Finger

4th D, D♭, A, A♭
FFcP

Let's give that pinky a REAL workout! This may be a new way to do a D scale, but learn this, and only one fret down gives you the base for a C♯ scale!

Extra Credit:
Move all four exercises up a string, and do the keys of G, F, E♭, and A. The fingering is identical! Move everything up one fret, and do the keys of C♯, B, A, and E♭.

11

Practice Hints

Use a metronome.

Repeat signs are not arbitrary. Repeat the selections within these bars as often as you need to make them comfortable. You can't overplay them!

Tempo is determined by how fast you can play the hardest sections (4ths!) comfortably and with good tone. "Swing" the notes, and connect them as smoothly as possible. Make the top of the mandolin resonate conceptually the whole time you are playing.

Use a metronome.

You might not be use to voicing patterns in intervals of **4th**s, but this is good for your ear and foreign to the mandolin. It will give you an "edgier," contemporary sound to your improvisation.

In the chord tone (**I vi7 ii7 V7**) and "approach tone" section, think music theory. Engage your brain in analyzing the scale degrees, so when you apply the patterns to improvisation, you're able to consciously define the scale degrees.

Did we mention, use a metronome?

Use the "home" pattern (straight major scale) as a kind of mental "rest area" so that you can leave fingers on "auto-pilot" and think about what you're doing in advance of the harder sections.

Hold the fingers close to the strings and over the fret positions in a "stand-by" stance when they aren't playing a note. Readiness is key to keeping the tone constant, the line sustained, and individual notes within the phrase well connected to each other.

Merits of FFcP

Flat keys are predominant in jazz. The so-called "horn keys" are a rarity in folk and bluegrass where open strings actually generate and direct harmony, form and structure in composition. The overtone series of sax, trumpet, and trombone, based in B♭ and E♭, made the use of flat keys much more common, which will demand greater frequency and use of 6th fret (pinky) on the mandolin.

Complexity and variety of tonal "micro-centers:" Jazz is notorious for its harmonic variety and lush chromaticism. It's not unusual to weave in and out of the overall key of the song with multiple, defining tonic departures. The ability to shift in and out of several keys in one song is crucial.

Transposability of the FFcP up and down the fretboard: Learn them in the lower positions, the harmonic relationships move identically into the higher frets, as well as across the strings.

4th finger strength and flexibility: Calisthenics work muscles that get used infrequently. Conceive of the "over-use" of the pinky in these exercises as an opportunity to develop coordination that needs extra attention.

General Starting Positions: One Octave FFcP Major Scales

STARTING	4th string-G	3rd String-D	2nd String-A	1st String-E
FRET	1st FFcP	1st FFcP	1st FFcP	XX
1	Ab	Eb	Bb	XX
	1st FFcP	1st FFcP	1st FFcP	XX
2	A	E	B	XX
	2nd FFcP	2nd FFcP	XX	XX
3	Bb	F	XX	XX
	2nd/3rd FFcP	2nd/3rd FFcP	XX	XX
4	B/Cb*	F#/Gb*	XX	XX
	3rd FFcP	3rd FFcP	XX	XX
5	C	G	XX	XX
	3rd/4th FFcP	4th FFcP	XX	XX
6	C#/Db*	Ab	XX	XX
	4th FFcP	4th FFcP	XX	XX
7	D	A	XX	XX
FIFTH: *(Station 2)*	4th string-G	3rd String-D	2nd String-A	1st String-E
	1st FFcP	1st FFcP	1st FFcP	XX
5	C	G	D	XX
	1st FFcP	1st FFcP	1st FFcP	XX
6	C#/Db	Ab	E	XX
SEVENTH: *(Station 3)*	4th string-G	3rd String-D	2nd String-A	1st String-E
	1st FFcP	1st FFcP	1st FFcP	XX
7	D	A	E	XX
	1st FFcP	1st FFcP	1st FFcP	XX
8	Eb	Bb	F	XX
	2nd FFcP	2nd FFcP	2nd FFcP	XX
9	E	B	F#	
	2nd FFcP	2nd FFcP	XX	XX
10	F	C	XX	XX
	3rd/2nd FFcP	3rd/2nd FFcP	XX	XX
11	F#/Gb	Db/C#	XX	XX
	3rd FFcP	3rd FFcP	XX	XX
12	G	D	XX	XX
	4th FFcP	4th FFcP	XX	XX
13	Ab	Eb	XX	XX
	4th FFcP	4th FFcP	XX	XX
14	A	E	XX	

*Note:
More often than not, some of the flat keys, especially Cb, Db, Gb, would use the latter position. The general principle for these flat keys, move the FFcP Down, Sharp a key, move the position up.
Lower position Cb and Gb would be conceptually better with the 3rd FFcP; Lower position Db would be conceptually better with the 4th FFcP.

Understand you are not limited to the above fingerings! The chart is based on three "wrist station" possibilities: low (open) position, 5th fret and 7th fret. You can start almost anywhere you can finish the octave.

You can also transpose these up even higher than the 12th fret, if your instrument and your own playing proficiency can handle it.

Moving the FFcP
up the Fingerboard

By now, you should be pretty intimate with the variations of the four basic **FFcP** positions. If you haven't already, you should be playing these variations not only down a fret and/or down a string, but also starting everything up on the higher frets.

For example, your **1st FFcP** in the key of A could move up and start on the 7th fret, and you would be using the same scale degree relationships only now in the key of D. The only new challenge would be tackling the "closeness" of the higher, narrower frets-eliminating the obnoxious buzzing or "near misses" of a poorly placed left-hand finger.

Particularly difficult is the 4th finger, as you worked so hard to strengthen and stretch in the lower frets. Now the challenge isn't so much strength as it is accuracy.

SLOW it down! Work on a clean, bell-like pick articulation. A clear, crisp attack is a crucial start, but that golden sustain can only happen when you find the magic "sweet spot" between the frets.

Work into your practice routine, all four **FFcP**, starting on the 5th and 7th frets (6th & 8th too). After weeks of getting comfortable with this, it's time to work on a smooth transition between the positions.

This next exercise, we will combine four **FFcP** in an attempt to work on shifting positions. We'll use six patterns and 2 different keys. The goal is to make the transition as seamless as possible, connect the patterns as if they were one.

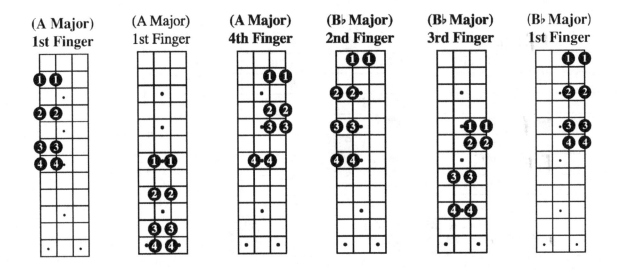

You might want to review the "Ionian Mandology" patterns again shown above. Once you're comfortable with them you can focus on the task at hand: a comfortable, confident shift from **FFcP** to **FFcP**! Now it's time for "Moving on Up…"

Moving on Up

Demonstrating the FFcP Potential
Transposing the positions up the fingerboard
IMPORTANT: PLAY AS TABBED!

FFcP up the neck

This exercise is to start you thinking about moving your FFcP shapes up the fretboard. **Some of the position shifts are purely academic,** but demonstrate how easy it is to transpose the four basic shapes. Once you start to feel comfortable with these, it's time to leave the safety of the lower frets and discover new scale degree relationships above the 5th fret and beyond.

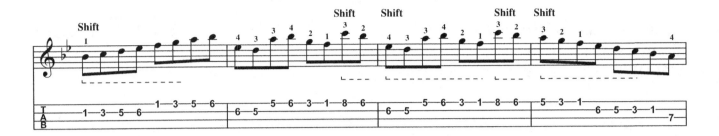

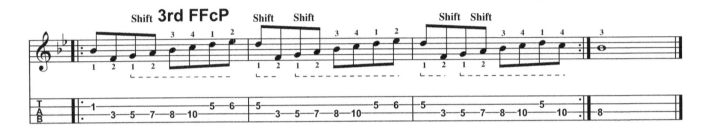

Notice you have used all four positions. When these relationships soak in, you'll notice you don't even have to think about what key you are in—it's all about scale degree function.

This is just the major scale, but once you master these, it's easy to tackle the minor modes, and some modal variations. Try **lowering the seventh scale degree** (G♯ to G in the first key, and A to A♭ in the second, B♭). Another interesting variation would be to **raise the 4th scale degree** (D to D♯ in the first key, A, and E♭ to E natural in the second, B♭)

Measures 11-13 and 25-27 are purely for understanding and feeling the position shift. Try to make these position changes quickly, but smooth, keeping your left wrist relaxed. The goal is for the move to be undetectable by the listener.

Avoid playing with any tension, you want to conceptualize your left wrist arriving securely at its station; practice these motions even without actually playing the notes out loud, just to get a feel for where your wrist needs to land behind the neck.

*Think of each position as a "hotel." You want to be secure and comfortable in the **FFcP** you are planted, but you want to have your "reservations" made for the next hotel. You need to transport efficiently from one hotel to the next, not wasting time in the transition to the next...*

The Secret of the Half Steps

Scales are a sequence of half steps and whole steps. A simple review: a half step on the mandolin is one fret, a whole step is two frets. An "interval" is the distance between the scale degrees.

Where the whole-steps are broken up by half steps determines what kind of scale. The major scale is whole, whole, half, whole, whole, whole, half. The intervals in frets would be **2 frets, 2 frets, 1 fret, 2 frets, 2 frets, 2 frets, 1 fret**.

You could spell this all out on one string, but it's unnecessary, as the next string duplicates the 7th fret. You finish the second half of the scale on the next string up without having to shift positions.

Scale Degree Relationships: A Major Scale

This is how the scale would lay out if you started on the key of **A** on the lowest string:

Notice the intervals, two frets, two frets, one fret is repeated in the second half of the scale. This is one of the greatest features of our eight stringed wonder, the "symmetry" of the instrument. As you explore these relationships, you'll want to identify and engrain them into your playing physically (fingers), aurally (ear), and intellectually (brain).

Another "trick" you'll want to absorb is the *location* of the half steps. These two pairs are a key ingredient (pun intended) of expressing the tonality in two different ways, the **key notes** and the **gravity notes**.

(A Major)
1st Finger

Key notes (also "Guide Tones"):
The **3rd** and **1st** (or **8th**) are what define "major-ness" (or "minor-ness") and tonal center (root). If the distance between 2 and 3 were a half step, it would be minor; between 2 and 3 a whole step (two frets) it would be major.

The **1st** (or **8th**) is "ground" zero, also known as the **root**. This is the **tonal center**.

Gravity notes:

The 7th degree is only a half step (one fret) beneath the **8th** (**1st**). This is the strongest melodic "pull" in Western (European) Music. Start your scale from 1, ascend all the way to seven but stop before you get to 8, and you hear that pull. It wants to go there, like a falling rock wants to hit the ground. This is why we'll call this a "gravity" note.

The second strongest pull is the **4th** degree, which is a half step (one fret) above the 3rd. It "pulls" in the other direction; it wants to go down. Doing so not only resolves tension, it establishes the "major-ness" of the music.

The Secret of the Half steps!

Now you'll discover the "secret" of the half steps. Marking these mentally and physically will allow your music to play in and out of tension and resolution within the key center. You can think of it as a sort of game of musical chairs. You can run around the notes like chairs in the game, but when the music is supposed to stop, you must land on a chair (guide tone) and not a gravity note, or you won't have the "rest" or release of tension the ear yearns for. Meander all you want, but make sure you are headed for one of these tones, the **1st** or **3rd** ("Key notes" or "Guide Tones").

When improvising, you can "play" with the tension even more by taunting and teasing with the gravity notes **4th** and **7th**, but remember, you are playing with fire! They want to pull to their respective positions of peace.

As you get into extended harmonies of chord extensions like **9ths**, **11ths**, and **13ths**, it gets more complicated, but in the early stages, concentrate on finding the half steps. This also helps you build your familiarity with all the scale patterns.

(B♭ Major) **(C Major)** **(D Major)**
2nd Finger **3rd Finger** **4th Finger**

The mandolin is perfect for grasping this. Actually any instrument tuned in **5ths** gives you this access; one or both of the notes in the pairs will always be one string up. Identify this immediately and you'll be able to add the other notes (**2nd**, **6th**) into this comprehension.

Examine your other **FFcP** positions for where the half steps occur. Find your own mental pattern to absorb this, and you'll take to improvisation like a duck to water.

The **2nd FFcP** may be the most difficult since you have a string crossing separating the two pairs, but even the awareness of that can help you work out melodies more effectively

The following exercise can help you develop this sense in all **12 keys** and 4 **FFcPs**. Connect the notes, paying particularly close attention the pull of the **4** to **3**, and **7** to **1**.

Guides and Gravity
A 'Circle of Fifths' approach in learning all 12 keys.

 Track #6

Diatonic Linear Gravity:

7 pulls to 1

4 pulls to 3

6 pulls to 5

2 pulls to 1

Start off SLOWLY!

CONSIDER EACH TWO MEASURE SET AS A SEPARATE STUDY. Don't be afraid to overwork each individual key. **CONNECT THE NOTES AS CLOSELY AS POSSIBLE.** Hold the tone as long as you can before the articulation of the following note. *("Breathe" it like a clarinet, not a mandolin...)*

USE THE FIRST MEASURE OF EACH PAIR TO SET THE KEY MENTALLY. The drill is in the following measure, so note the scale degrees—how each micro "resoluton" relates to the tonic. (i.e. 4th to 3rd, 7th to 1st, 6th to 5th)

SPEED IS NOT AS IMPORTANT AS FUNCTION RECOGNITION. Focus on where the scale tones resolve.

Arpeggios: Subconscious Melodic Roadmaps

The tendency for most players who study **scales** intensely is to play the notes consecutively, in **stepwise** motion, up and down. The problem with stopping there, is that good music actually skips around. It punches in, out, and around, but ultimately emphasizes the so called "good" notes, the chord tones of **1st, 3rd, 5th, 7th** and the extensions.

Not only does it skip occasionally, it also mixes up **direction**; just like the law of gravity: what goes up must come down. The ear likes this variety and it's good to plant in your subconscious, **patterns** that allow you to "autopilot" your improvisation. It also helps to label them mentally in groups of notes, as your music "vocabulary" is spoken in sentences, rather than words.

Even when reading this paragraph, you will probably connect familiar phrases intellectually, because you are so used to seeing them in combinations. You rarely think of an individual word (unless it's new or unfamiliar); you usually think in much bigger strokes than that.

Now we need to go beyond **scales**; not give them up, but *add* to them. Hopefully, you've had a chance to work the preceding **FFcP** scales into tactile intimacy. The goal is to know them so well, you can forget them. Your fingers don't, but your brain foregoes them for higher function melodic development. (If you had a third arm, you could drink a cup of coffee while playing them...)

> The goal is to know scales so well, you can forget them.

Introducing: 7th Chord Arpeggios

The next section takes some common **7th chord** arpeggios and lets you drill them into your fingers and into the fretboard. This can be a part of your daily regimen. As you master them, you'll want to revisit them as warm-ups, perhaps one day on major, one day on minor, etc.

This section of the book is on **melodic** development, but note that we can't separate **melodic** from **harmonic** (chords) here. We are spelling out chords, after all. The purpose of these exercises is more to build your skills in improvisation, so we've intentionally mixed them up a bit. There is an overall pattern, four measures with each measure progressing up in 3rds, each set of four progressing backwards in the circle of 5ths, but that is moot! (Forget I pointed that out...) The idea is to comprehensively cover all combinations, but not necessarily have a mental association from measure to measure. Think of it more as arpeggio "flash cards."

Don't lose the discipline of the **FFcP** closed fingering combinations. As you digest them first in your fingers, later into your ears, you'll start making the mental association that will empower you to move them all up and down the fretboard.

Most important: Make them pretty! Don't lose the concept of good tone, sustain, and note connection.
Remember: it's what goes on between the notes that produces good line!

Maj7 Arpeggios

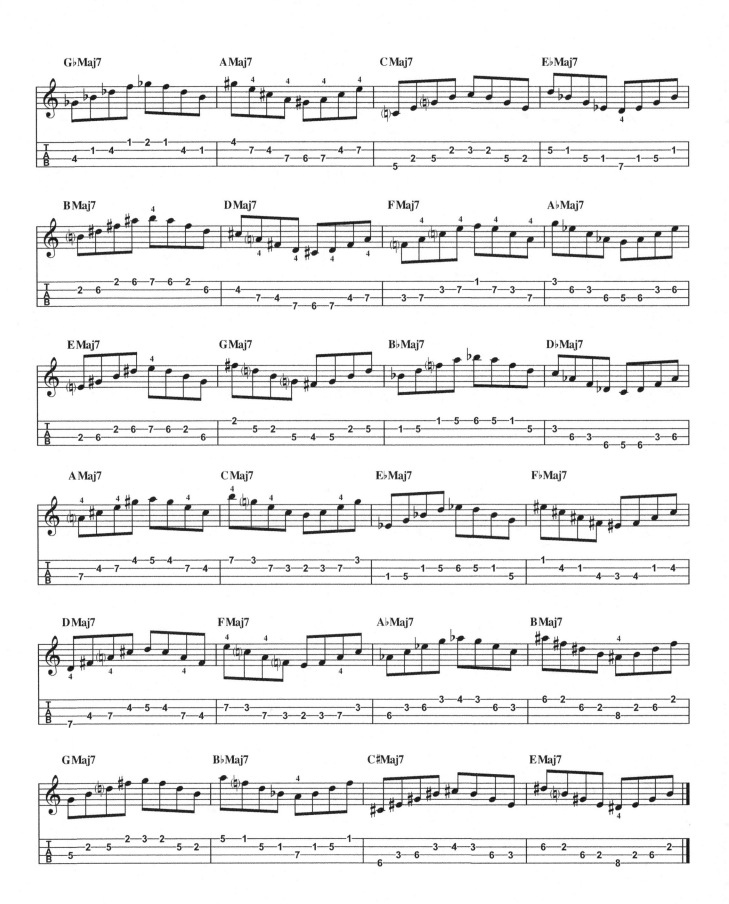

22

Dom7 Arpeggios

Min7 Arpeggios

Track #9

25

Min6 Arpeggios

Minor 6th and Half Diminished 7ths Chords (m7♭5)
Just a bit of gypsy...

In our efforts to reduce the number of harmonic possibilities, it's important to acknowledge a fantastic short-cut. You can woodshed for hours, the possibilities of chording or arpeggiating the **Minor 6th** chord, only to find that all the notes are identical to the Half Diminished chord, more commonly called the **m7♭5**, or Minor 7th chord with a flatted 5th, based on a root a 3rd scale degree away.

Chord Duplication: Cm6 = C, E♭, G, A and Am7♭5 = A, C, Eb, G

For example a **Cm6** includes the notes, **C, E♭, G, A**. If you invert the same sequence of notes starting with A, you would have an **Am7♭5**, or **A, C, E♭, G**. The difference in context would be what the bass note is playing. If you can recognize the four note interval relationship, you don't have to learn 12 additional arpeggios or chords, just ONE relationship!

Chord Transposition Reference Chart				
ROOT	**m6 chord**		**ROOT**	**m7 5**
A	Am6	=	F♯/G♭	F♯m7♭5
B♭	B♭m6	=	G	Gm7♭5
B	Bm6	=	A♭/G♯	G♯m7♭5
C	Cm6	=	A	Am7♭5
C♯/D♭	C♯m6	=	B♭	B♭m7♭5
D	Dm6	=	B/C♭	Bm7♭5
E♯/D♭	E♭m6	=	C	Cm7♭5
E	Em6	=	C♯/D♭	C♯m7♭5
F	Fm6	=	D	Dm7♭5
F♯/G♭	F♯m6	=	E♭/D♯	E♭m7♭5
G	Gm6	=	E	Em7♭5
A♭/G♯	A♭m6	=	F	Fm7♭5

Yet another trick up our sleeve is the issue of **Dominant** 9th chords. A **Rootless Dominant** 9th (F9 without the F) is the same as a **m7♭5** chord based on the 3rd scale degree (Am7♭5). Knowing these patterns is invaluable in communicating the Dominant Function forms.

In other words, we have reduced three specific functions into one set of arpeggios:

Chord notes: C, E♭, G, A
Minor 6th = Minor 7th (♭5) = Rootless 9th
Cm6 **Am7♭5** **F9(no F)**

This is a great incentive to practice these patterns; they are also extremely common in the harmonic language of Gypsy Jazz, Bebop, and Brazilian Jazz.

Lydian DUDU

Major Scale with a raised 4th
Important: Maintain Down-Up-Down-Up picking "flow" throughout…

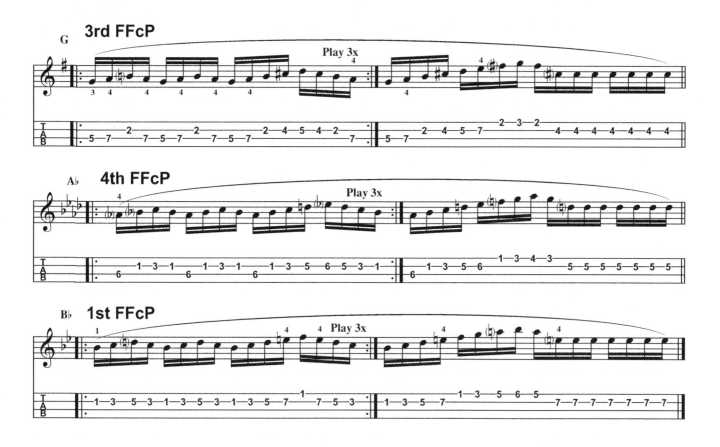

Play each two to four times before moving on to the next key. Work on an even, smooth tone, especially between string crossings.

1.) Keep the left-hand fingers close to the fingerboard so as to connect each note. (This is a terrific stretching exercise!)

2.) Maintain a DUDU (Down-Up-Down-Up) stroke, relaxing the right-hand wrist. (Clear, full wrist stroke yielding volume with no tension.)

3.) Remember where your scale degrees are; think 1, 2, 3, 2, 1, 2, 3, 2, etc. and "raised 4" in each position (Think of the pattern as a major scale with a raised 4th scale degree.)

4.) Practice it two ways: straight sixteenths, and swing sixteenths.

5.) Feel free to add the keys in between the printed keys.

6.) Experiment with moving the FFcP up the fretboard.

This is an excellent warm-up for RH wrist and LH fingers. Focus on creating maximum, full tone with crisp, bell-like snap of the pick, a full stroke of the wrist, and a sustained duration connecting every note.

31

Melodic Improvisational Concepts
Building off a Simple Major scale

If you've played the mandolin (or perhaps another instrument) for a while, you are probably very familiar with several major scales. The purpose in drilling **FFcP** fingerings is to make you comfortable beyond the few "Fiddle" or Folk keys, like **G, D, A,** or **C** and establish a tactile road map for extending your access to the other keys such as **A♭, E♭, B♭,** what we might call the "horn" keys, or even the "Jethro" keys. When you finally do get comfortable with these major key patterns *(in all 12 keys!)*, it's time to go to the next level and start building alterations of the major scale.

You'll discover later in the text as we unravel the concept of "**tonal centers,**" that knowing which key center you are in at any given time gives you immediate improvisational fodder with the major (or minor) key of that area. We'll go into more detail later, but we'll stick with the linear or melodic opportunities for the time being.

In the previous exercise, the **Lydian DUDU,** we took the excuse of developing Right Hand/Left Hand finger coordination and tone development, and introduced you to a new sound. We took a simple **FFcP** pattern and **raised the 4th scale degree**.

For the Folk Musician "ear," this was probably as much a stretch as the fingering was. However this scale gives you a new tonal flavor with a lot of applications. If you were playing "Modal" Jazz, where instead of confronting multiple tonal centers and complex chord changes, you play 6 or 10 measures of the same chord, sticking to the major scale might sound dull. Raising the **4th** scale degree adds a "tension" that can entice the ear in these situations.

The scale is referred to as the "**Lydian**" scale in some circles. Without confounding you with a slew of new labels, let's just say this is a scale based on one of the Western (European) Music Church Modes. The label is not important, but the sound certainly is.

We'll take the opportunity now to practice a tune that will use two of these scales. Note in its simplicity, there is plenty of melodic opportunity for fresh creativity, just by altering one note, and only playing in two keys.

Lydia O'Lydia

Major scale with a raised 4th

Ted Eschliman

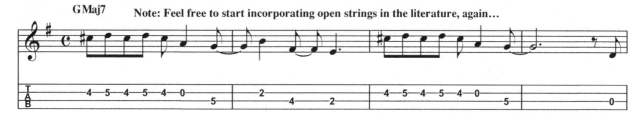

More Modal Considerations

Jazz theory texts will take you through extensive and exhaustive explorations of modes, based on different notes of the major and minor scale. For some, this is a way of getting one's arms around certain improvisational concepts. For practical purposes, we won't go beyond a casual mention of these modes. If you're coming from the Bluegrass or Folk genres, which dominate North American mandolin playing, you are already used to the **Major Scale**. As a shortcut, we will only explore a couple modes, but reference them as a variation of the major scale.

We just learned the **Lydian** mode (although you didn't really know the name of it). Starting a major scale from the **4th** scale degree yields this mode, which coincidentally is the major scale with its W, W, **H**, W, W, H step progression altered only one note, the **4th** scale degree, which we raised to create a new pattern. (W, W, **W**, H, W, W, H)

Now we'll learn another pattern, commonly called the **Dorian** mode. Based on the notes of the **2nd** degree of the major scale, its step relationship is W, H, W, W, H, W. It's the same as the Major Scale, except we lower the **3rd** and **7th** degrees.

The **3rd** degree of a chord or scale defines the "major or minor-ness" of the music. In the case of **Dorian**, it feels minor. The lowered 7th removes the gravitational pull of the leading tone and adds its own element of "wander" or "ramble" to the sound. This character was well developed in the post-Bebop era when "**Modal Jazz**" was in its heyday in the mid 20th century.

A reaction to Bebop's blistering pyrotechnics and fast harmonic changes, **Modal Jazz** would stay on one chord longer to explore different elements of melodic development. This offers a great opportunity for beginning jazz mandolinists to further their skills on one chord. The ability to make that one chord interesting is quite a challenge in itself. Let's develop a little familiarity with the **Dorian** scale.

Since you already know the major scale well, you don't need to spend vast amounts of time on stepwise (consecutive note) drilling. Your attention to daily **FFcP** scales will give you that. The next exercise introduces not only the characteristic sounds of the Dorian mode, it breaks the scale up with an arpeggiated approach. Starting with the top note of a triad note chord is a fresh way to tackle this. It's easy to get trapped by starting every improvisation on the root of the chord. These start with the 5th scale degree.

*A fringe benefit to the following exercise is developing a syncopated feel. The way the notes should be phrased and implied accent on the first of three 8th notes gets you away from the static **1 & 2 & 3 & 4 &** subdivision. This is another "feel" that you should develop. Don't lose the DUDU (alternating down/up) picking, but at the same time, feel a natural emphasis even though some of them are an upstroke.*

Dorian Patterns

Dorian Patterns, descending by 4ths
Minor 3rd, but Major 6th and Minor 7th

* Play each two measure sequence as many times as it takes to feel comfortable before moving to the next.
* Don't deviate from **DUDU** (down up) picking articulation, but feel free to accent the alternating upstrokes that start each slur.
* Think Dorian center key, but also think the (key signature) of the major scale (whole step below) it is related to.

Dorian's Grey

Major scale with a lowered 3rd and 7th or
Minor scale with lowered 7th and raised 6th

Ted Eschliman

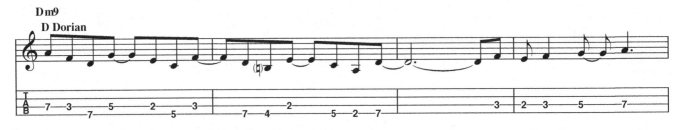

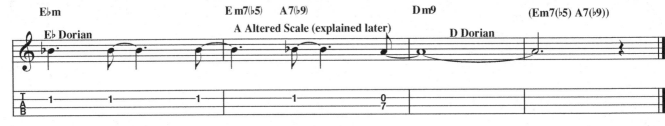

Dorian scales to base improvisation or in the above song:

A Little bit of Gypsy
The Aug 11th Scale

A common trick of **Django** or "**Gypsy**" jazz, is to take a **Major** scale with a lowered **7th** scale degree (otherwise known as the Mixolydian Mode) and play around with the **4th** scale degree. If you've played Bluegrass or Celtic music (or even Blues for that matter), you are already familiar with the effect of **lowering the 7th scale degree.**

You've probably already experimented with that sound; in folk music, if you see a **dominant 7th chord** like G7, you just naturally lower the 7th scale degree to fit the chord. Instead of using an F♯, you plug in an F natural, which IS the **Mixolydian Mode.**

The next bit of flavor is to raise the 4th just like we did in the Lydian mode, but keep the lowered 7th. This is a very playful, restless palette of sound to paint with.

You'll also experience the charm of this sound south of the equator in Brazilian music; from Choro to the music of Jobim, you'll hear this extension of the **Dominant 7th** chord take on a whole new dimension.

One way to understand this is to think of the notes of the dominant 7th chord with its consecutive passing tones, but as we extend the V7 chord up, adding a **9th**, and an **11th** note, we see how the raised 11th note spices up the dominant chord. The **4th** and **11th** are actually the same note, but for clarity purposes, you'll see it referred to as an **Augmented 11th** (+11, ♯11).

It's getting ahead of ourselves right now, but later we'll cover the **Altered Scale**, which will share identical relationships with the Augmented 11th Scale, but start on a different note, the 4th. It will share what we will call the **Tri-tone** substitution role, but don't worry about that right now. The important thing is digging more "ruts' in your fretboard that make these patterns automatic. We only mention this in passing as extra justification for internalizing these. (You'll encounter them again.)

Another contemporary convention unique to jazz is breaking away from intervals in **3rds** and using **4ths**. It doesn't lay quite as easily on the mandolin fretboard, but it's an excellent way of adding jazz "dialect" to your playing. We're going to explore the **Aug 11th** scale this way in the next exercise. Feel free, however to practice your **FFcP** scale patterns using the raised 4th and lowered 7th on your own.

In later 20th century jazz styles, any time you see a **V7** chord, this scale is almost always fair game!

"Berklee Gypsy" Drills

Focus on connecting the notes

3rd C, C♯, G, A♭
FFcP

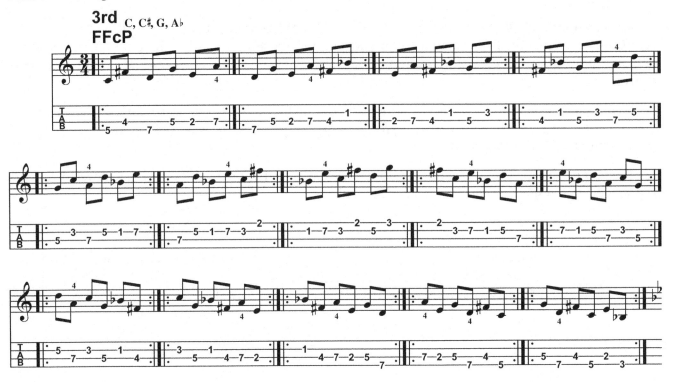

Broken 4ths can give you a very "contemporary" sound

2nd B♭, B, F, F♯
FFcP

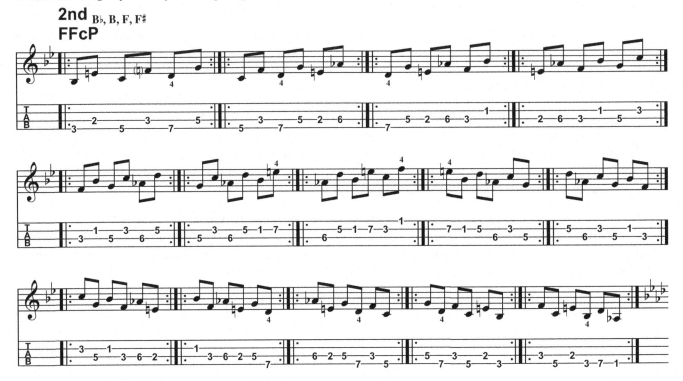

Conceptualize the Aug 11th scale as a Major scale with a lowered 7th and a raised 4th degree.

Repeat Signs are not arbitrary. Repeat the selections within the bars as often as you need to make them comfortable. Don't progress from one measure to the next until played cleanly.

Be sure to familiarize yourself with the pattern in all 12 keys.

1st Ab, A, Eb, E
FFcP

Note the Aug 11th scale can work beautifully in context of dominant chord, especially in Bebop, Gypsy Jazz, Western Swing, and Bazilian Choro.

4th D, Db, Ab, A
FFcP

The Altered Scale

Leaving the safety and complacency of the diatonic world for the edgier vocabulary of the Bebop jazz musician.

Symmetrical Scales

The Altered Scale is fertile fodder for the consummate Bebop musician. Unlike previous scales in this book, this borrows from a different category of scales, completely outside of the variations on Major or Minor scales. A whole new category of contemporary scales called symmetrical scales.

Diminished and Whole Tone:

Borrowing from these symmetrical scales, the Diminished (1/2, W, 1/2, W, 1/2, W, 1/2, W) and the Whole Tone (W, W, W, W, W, W), two 'Tetrachords' (four-note patterns) are spliced together to make the culinary equivalent of a chocolate fudge, French vanilla swirl ice cream cone. (1/2, W, 1/2, W, W, W, W).

To the diehard Bluegrass musician or anyone whose feet are permanently planted in the 'diatonic' or modal world, this is going to be quite foreign in feel and sound. It may take your ears (let alone fingers) some getting used to, but if you listen to any Coltrane, Parker, Rollins, it may be familiar. Now, you're going to be able to pick apart what they do, and reproduce it on the fretboard!

D Altered Scale in 4 FFcP Positions:

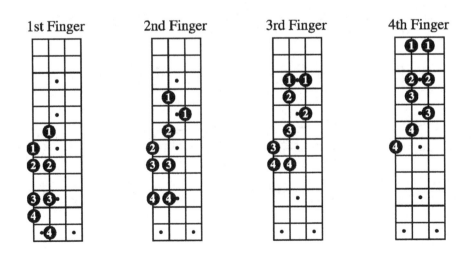

Where is it used?

Jazz is all about **tension** and **resolution**. By itself, the **Altered Scale** is quite a "tense" sound, so its best application is whenever you have a **Dominant Functioning Chord** (V7, V7 plus extensions, diminished chord, augmented). Used judiciously (and deliciously!) this can be a spicy concoction to give you the recipe for authentic jazz. This will set you apart from ANY Bluegrass-saturated jazz wannabe.

How do I learn them?

You can play them raw, but what you need to start on immediately is "context." Rarely in music do we play eight notes in linear succession, except in dramatic runs. You want this to be practical. We've developed an exercise, **Bebop Mandology**, that takes them in their four note *(tetrachord)* chunks, and mixes the direction, and works this into your brain (and fingers) as dynamically tactile patterns.

In closed position (no open strings), there are only four, one-octave (**FFcP**) patterns, starting with each finger. This will give you the chance to work all four fingerings in the same exercise. Also, because this pattern is best used in a **Dominant Function** context, you have the opportunity to work these through in the **Circle of Fifths**. There are only twelve, and you start all over again!

> *There are a lot of "**Circle of Fifth**" inclusive Standards out there you could insert these patterns into! Sweet Georgia Brown, I've Got Rhythm (bridge), Scrapple from Apple (bridge), All of Me, as examples.*

Exercise Variations:

Practice Suggestions for Bebob Mandology:

*Play it straight, repeat the whole exercise… Indefinitely. Until the cows come home.

*Play each measure, but repeat before going to the next measure.

*Play two measures, repeat in two measure patterns.

*Play every other measure. Go back, start with the 2nd measure and play every other measure.

*Play the first half of the measure as written, but the second half as intervals (3rds).

*Play the first half of the measure as intervals (3rds), but the second half as written. (See above "**Exercise Variations**")

 **Track #16**

Bebop Mandology
(Dim Whole Dom Cycle)

Breaking beyond Bluegrass into the
Bebop vocabulary

The Altered Scale (a.k.a. Diminished

Whole tone, Super-Locran, Pomeroy)

Ted Eschliman

*The purpose of the above exercise is to acquaint you with one octave finger patterns of the **Altered Scale**. You will hear it in context with the "Minor in Possession" following exercise. The above runs you through the Cycle of fifths, so it's important you begin to develop a "second nature" sense of the dominant (V) relationships.*

Be sure to incorporate the three variations listed in the previous page! Mix them up, eventually.

Note: we introduce another "Gravity Note," the ♭9, which resolves to the 5th of I.

*The 4th note of each series has been spelled enharmonically, for simplicity's sake. In the first measure, though the key (E) would feature a G♯, we'll use A♭ so as to show eight distinct steps.

Minor in Possession

Introducing the Altered Scale!
'V7 (alt) - I' resolutions to minor tonic.

Be aware of the scale degree relationships and resolutions in each 2nd measure.

One small step for a mandolin, one giant leap from a G Chop…

Minor: V7(♭9) i

 Track #21

Using the Altered Scale:
The minor key and its Dominant (V7)

45

See the following pages for chord fingering suggestions.

Try to establish a mental as well as physical (tactile) relationships with the "**Altered Scale**" based on the **Dominant (V7) chord**, yet remain conscious of the minor key each two measure pattern is based on.

Minor Cadences: V7(♭9) i

Chord possibilities for the V7 I in minor keys, using the ♭9 extension on the V7, i.e. E7(♭9).

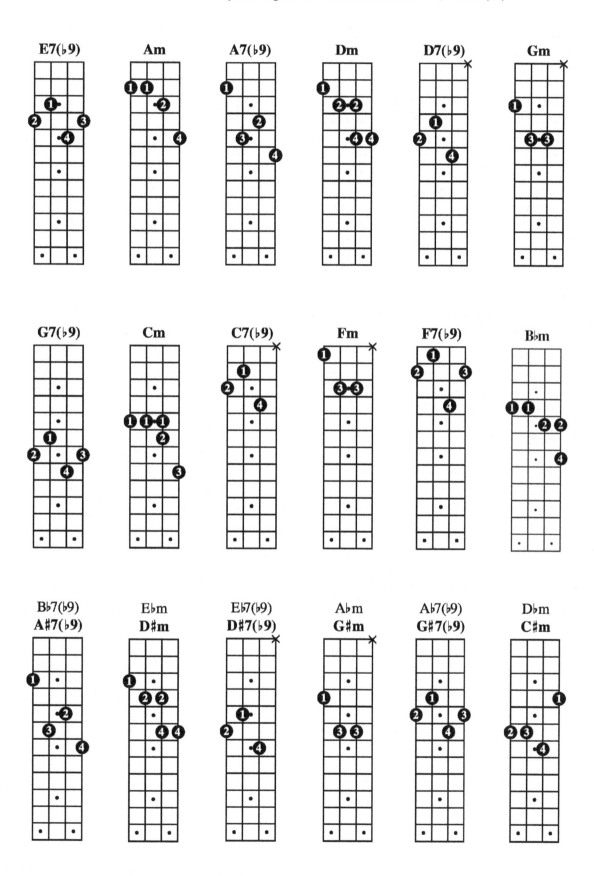

Minor Cadences: V7(♭9) i *(cont'd)*

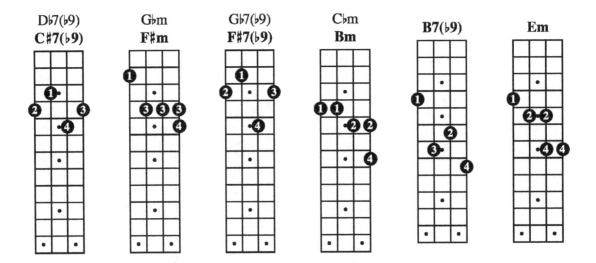

Db7(♭9) C♯7(♭9) | Gbm F♯m | Gb7(♭9) F♯7(♭9) | Cbm Bm | B7(♭9) | Em

Enharmonic Equivalents:

Note that some of the above enharmonic equivalents are only hypothetical. Gb minor and Cb minor exist in theory; nonetheless, they may exist as tonal centers, and should be part of your chord vocabulary.

Transposition of Patterns:

The preceding chords are suggestions. You have the flexibility of moving them up and down the fretboard, so experiment with simple transpositions up or down a fret or two. Once they become comfortable and familiar, you will find yourself doing just that.

Different Extensions:

The emphasis here has been on the (♭9) extension of the dominant seventh chord. You can experiment with your own chords and voicings by substituting (+9) or adding (♭13) or (+11). Consider the **Dominant 7th** as a jumping off point for more of your own chords. You can also experiment with variations on the tonic (**I**) chord by adding the **9th** scale degree (im9), or even a raised **6th** (im6) scale degree.

Using the Altered Scale for the Dominant Chord of a Minor key:

The purpose of using the (♭9) extension here is to familiarize you with the sound and use of the **Altered Scale.** The preceding exercise gives you the opportunity to use this scale within this context. Being able to move back and forth between melodic improvisations on these chords is another way to reinforce tactile positions.

Take the opportunity to think of the association between dominant function and the notes of the Altered Scale. This will give you immediate fodder for melodic improvisation when you encounter these tonal centers.

Chord and Melody: Transition

Switching back and forth from Chording to Melodic Playing

Chord melody playing is one of the most challenging skills to tackle on a mandolin, but once mastered, it can be the most satisfying of musical experiences. All-in-one, you can sketch the harmonic structure of a piece, yet maintain the melodic flow. In the best of both worlds, the ensemble is reduced to one singular instrument, a "Band in a Box."

The advanced art of **chord melody** is beyond the scope of this book, but we can certainly start you down that road. The first step is to be able to switch seamlessly from straight chording to single note melody playing. This skill establishes the tonal centers, and also lays out the essential ingredients of good improvisation and melody building.

We've dabbled at this with '**V7(♭9) i**' cadences, but now we'll infuse the rich vocabulary of the **Altered Scale** and some spicy syncopation. This also gives you the opportunity to practice rhythmic variety in your (chord) comping. This involves as much focus on left-hand control as picking in that the degree of muting or "choking" the chord allows you to let the chord ring for harmonic definition, or "chop" for rhythmic.

> Tag the V7 association, the Dominant/Tonic relationship in your mind as you play these.

The right hand should maintain a steady **DUDU** (*Down Up Down Up*) metronomic flow. Even when the chord is not picked, the subdivided (eighth note) articulation keeps the beat steady and puts the degree of "chunk vs. ring" into the left-hand fingers.

If you're not already doing it, "tag" the **V7** association, the **Dominant/Tonic** relationship in your mind as you play these. If you're in A minor, E7 needs to coexist in the front of your thinking.

Again, don't feel like you need to plow through the whole exercise. Reduce it to bite sized chunks. Don't move from one key center to the next until you've comfortably mastered the section. If digesting 12 keys at once is too overwhelming, limit it to two or three keys in one day.

You want a good tone, and precise articulation. Start down the road to planting these into your subconscious.

Prepared to Dominate…

Minor World Dominants

**Alternating Chord comping
with the Altered Scale**

Be conscious of each minor tonal center as you
progress through the Circle of Fifths!

50

51

Jazz Harmonic Function

"Who am I; Why am I here?"

(Admiral James Stockdale, 1992 Vice Presidential Debates)

```
┌─────────────────────────────────┐
│            Tonic                │
│  Major: I (Maj7, Maj6)          │
│  Minor: i (m9)                  │
└─────────────────────────────────┘
```

```
┌──────────────────────────────────────────────────────┐
│                    Dominant                          │
│  Major and Minor: V7 (V7♭9, V7+9, VAug7, V13, viim7♭5)│
└──────────────────────────────────────────────────────┘
```

```
┌─────────────────────────────────────┐
│      Dominant Preparation           │
│  Major: ii7, IV, vi7 (IVMaj7)       │
│  Minor: ii7♭5, iv                   │
└─────────────────────────────────────┘
```

```
┌──────────────────────────────────────────────────┐
│                  Hybrid                          │
│  Vsus7, iii7, ♭VII, any "sus" chord. X no 3rd   │
└──────────────────────────────────────────────────┘
```

Basic Notation Conventions to Help you understand:

Roman Numerals used in Scale Degrees (I through VII)
Upper Case designate Major chord; **I, II, III, IV, V, VI, VII**
Lower Case designate Minor chord; **i, ii, iii, iv, v (theoretical), vi, vii**

Seven three-note chords (triads) based on scale degrees:
Major: I ii iii IV V vi vii° I
Minor: i ii♭5 III iv V VI vii° i

Example **Key of A**:
Major: A Bm C♯m D E F♯m G♯dim A
Minor (Harmonic): Am Bdim C Dm E F G♯dim
(Note: no Alpha-numeric suffix implies major)

Key of A, diatonic 7th chords:
Major: AMaj7 Bm7 C♯m7 DMaj7 E7 F♯m7 G♯m7♭5 AMaj7
Minor (Harmonic): Am7 Bm7♭5 CMaj7 Dm7 E7 FMaj7 G♯m7♭5

One of the most efficient ways to develop jazz skills is to understand the concepts of **tension** and **resolution** that occur in chord function, based on the major (and minor) scale. You need to grasp them aurally (*hear* V to I), physically (*play* V to I), and ultimately, *intellectually* (knowing where the V is in all keys, and which tones resolve to their "partners" in tonic).

A good start is to know inside and out, the circle of fifths:

Go around the clock (clockwise); you'll see how each chord precedes the other as the 5th (V) of the key. We start at the 12:00 position with C; it is the 5th of F. F becomes the 5th of B♭, B♭ becomes the 5th of E♭, and so on around the clock.

We can't stress enough how automatic this needs to be. Every time you start a new key, the first note or chord you should identify needs to be the V, or V7 chord. Someone calls out "E Major," B7 (its V7) needs to be front and center in your thinking, as that V to I relationship is critical, even in bluegrass or folk music.

C G F
D B♭
A CICLE OF 5THS E♭
E A♭
B D♭
F♯

Tonic and Dominant Function:

This introduces us to the concept of **Tonic** and **Dominant Function**. The I chord is your **Tonic**, the V (V7) is your **Dominant**. Try playing through the following familiar chords, and use your ears to hear how they progress into each other:

E to A (E7 to A)
A to D (A7 to D)
G to C (G7 to C)
B to E (B7 to E)

These are all **Dominant** chords proceeding to **Tonic** chords. The second of the pair is the **Tonic** or home key. Let's also point out here that your key signature can help you in establishing the basic home key, but in jazz, you are not limited to one key. In most cases, you will flow through anywhere from 2 to 6 different keys or "tonal centers" in one song, so it's important to not necessarily think in terms of key signatures.

This is why your aural abilities are so important. You need to get away from the music intellectually sometimes and just use your ear to identify periods of tonal stability. Were you to stop the music in arbitrary places, can you identify what key you are in by singing it? Chances are, if you are at tonic, it was just "set up" by a preceding **Dominant**.

Dominant Alternative:

Notice the voicing of the triad in the 7th degree of the A Major scale, compared to the V7 chord:

viidim = G♯ B D (G♯dim)
V7 = E G♯ B D (E7)

They are identical, except for the E. This points out a strong alternative for the V, by merely dropping the root of the chord. The V is a fairly benign tone anyway, except when it's used in the bass, so you can use the diminished vii and V7 (or vii7♭5 and V9) interchangeably.

Dominant Preparation:

This concept allows a little more "liberty" in interpretation. Chords may set up or prepare the **Dominant** which ultimately resolves to a **Tonic**. While the **Dominant** is more limiting and arbitrary, the choices in chords that prepare for the **Dominant** are more abundant.

Chances are, if it's not a **Tonic** or **Dominant**, and you are still within the tonal center (not modulating to another key), you can lump this into the **Dominant Preparation** club. These would most likely be based on the **ii** and **IV** scale degrees, and once in a while, could be a **vi** or **iii** chord.

In **A Major**, the chords could be **Bm** (Bm7), **D** (DMaj7), or chords like **C♯m** and **F♯m**, all of which are chords based on the diatonic scale. Preceding or preparing for the **Dominant** to **Tonic** "statement" possibilities would be:

Bm E A
Bm7 E7 AMaj7
F♯m7 E7 AMaj7
F♯m7 Bm7 E7 AMaj6 *(two preparation chords)*

Notice it's the last two chords that define the key center aurally. No matter what you do to prepare, it's that E7 to A that really brings us home.

'ii V7 I' Cadence

Now we have the most common jazz "sentence." Take a listen to Bm7 E7 A, and you have all three ingredients, the **Dominant Preparation**, **Dominant**, and **Tonic**, in about as succinct a progression as you can make. State it, then get out of the way and listen. You ought to be able to clearly sing back the I or tonic, even without knowing what notes you just played. It's where the rubber meets the road.

Understand that working in this context allows you to freely define tonal centers and use the appropriate scales to base your improvisation on. Once you identify within the song where these tonal centers of **Prep**, **Dominant**, and **Tonic** are, you can implement the full diatonic scale of the progression.

If you are new at this, it might mean taking a pencil and marking where the key centers are. Using your ear first, identify where new keys are obvious. Then look for a **V** (or **vii**) chord to precede it. Working backwards, it will become obvious, which harmonic journey to base your solos on. Then it's as simple as playing the notes of the major (or minor) scale that **Tonal Center** is based on.

Secondary Dominants

We would be remiss in not mentioning that frequently NO preparation chord is used, and once in a while the Dominant actually leads to another Dominant. Take the progression from the classic "All of Me" in the **key of C**:

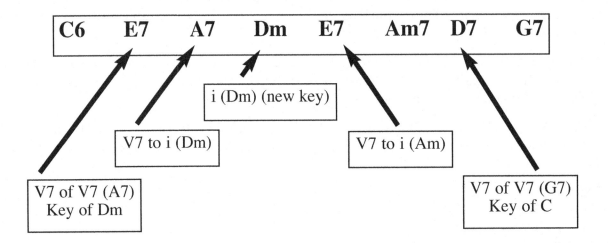

The first chord starts innocently enough in the **key of C**, but **E7**, the 2nd chord is not part of the key of C! Notice it leads to the **A7**, however which is the **V7** of **Dm**. We actually end the first four bars in the key of D minor.

Looking back, the **A7** is the **V7** of **D minor** (our new key) and **E7** is the **V7** of **A7**, so we'll label the **E7** a **Secondary Dominant**. It could be argued that A is for a microsecond a new tonal center, but its better not to split hairs and just call it the beneficiary of a **Secondary Dominant**.

The 2nd half of the phrase starts with a **V7** in a new temporary key center when **E7** goes to the **Am**. We see another secondary dominant **V of V** with the **D7** leading to the **G7** which eventually brings us back to the original key of **C Major**.

You may hear someone describe sections similar to this in other songs as **"Circle of Fifths"** because in essence, all you are doing is traveling the keys in descending 5ths, stacking dominant function after dominant function. The tonal centers are not completely settled, but you have the benefit of knowing what notes to play by virtue of knowing its function. We'll have exercises later in the book that will help develop this concept.

Hybrid

Hybrid chords are relatively new, and we don't need to explore them too much other than to say sometimes the function can be blurred. In the case of suspended or (**Sus4**) chords, they can be categorized as both **Preparation** and **Dominant**.

The 'ii V7 I'
The Essence of Jazz!

The **'ii V7 I'** is the most basic "sentence" of the harmonic (chordal) structure of jazz. Phrases end with this, keys modulate with this, and long static sections of music that linger on one chord can be supercharged with this progression. We cannot stress enough how critical it is you be intimately familiar with this pattern in all 12 keys.

An easy way to grasp this is to take 3 basic **Stock Patterns** and move them up and/or down 1, 2, or 3 frets. You have the benefit of a tactile familiarity, then it's just a matter of hooking up basic music theory (transposing) and moving this set of "relationships" up and down. Don't think **12 keys**; think **3 distinct patterns** moved slightly by a couple of frets.

Two different sets of the **Stock Patterns** need to be mastered, the **Major** and the **Minor**. It's easy to overlook the **Minor**, but try to get them into your fingers, too.

Notice a few of the following chords have a "9" in them, designating an added **9th** (or **2nd**) scale degree. This is simply a subjective style choice, and as the 9th is a fairly benign, non-tension tone, if can be added in most jazz genres, like a little salt on French Fries. However, you will need to be sensitive to other rhythm accompaniment players; if they are playing a chord voicing with a sharp or flat '9' (♯9, ♭9), you will want to stay out of the way. Generally, in smaller ensembles, it's not an issue.

Three-note chord patterns like the very first set are quite versatile. You can move them across the string, and you'll transpose the progression up one fifth:

Key of C: Dm7 G7 C *across one string* = Key of G: Am7 D7 G

Or you can substitute the muted string for extended chord voicings, like **9ths** (♯9, 9, ♭9), **11ths** (♯11), or **13ths** (13, ♭13) with the pinky. Many professionals use exclusively for this purpose, or just to retain a kind of "Old Time" purity staying away from the harmonic extensions.

The stock patterns are merely a "jumping off" point for you. Eventually, you'll develop variations of your own, ones that fit your personal style, and the music you choose to play. Don't be afraid to experiment!

> *Don't think **12 keys**; think **3 distinct patterns** moved slightly by a couple of frets.*

Sample Stock 'ii V7 I' Chord Fingerings
Major Patterns

Dm7

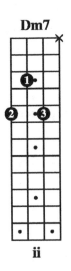

ii

G7

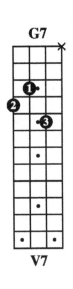

V7

C6/7

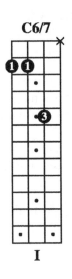

I

Key of C = Dm7 G7 C
-1 Key of B = C♯m7 F♯7 B
-2 Key of B♭ = Cm7 F7 B♭

Key of C = Dm7 G7 C
+1 Key of D♭ = E♭m7 A♭7 D♭
+2 Key of D = Em7 A7 D

Am7

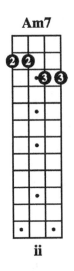

ii

D7

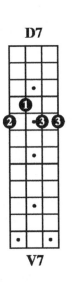

V7

GMaj9

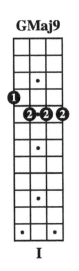

I

Key of G = Am7 D7 G
+1 Key of A♭ = B♭m7 E♭7 A♭
+2 Key of A = Bm7 E7 A
+3 Key of B♭ = Cm7 F7 B♭
+4 Key of B = C♯m7 F♯7 B
+5 Key of C = Dm7 G7 C

Fm9

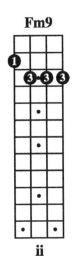

ii

B♭13

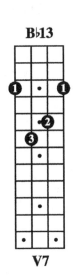

V7

E♭Maj9

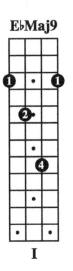

I

Key of E♭ = Fm7 B♭7 E♭
+1 Key of E = F♯m7 B7 E
+2 Key of F = Gm7 C7 F
+3 Key of F♯ = G♯m7 C♯7 F♯
+4 Key of G = Am7 D7 G
+5 Key of A♭ = B♭m7 E♭7 A♭

Sample Stock 'ii7♭5 V7 i' Chord Fingerings
Minor Patterns

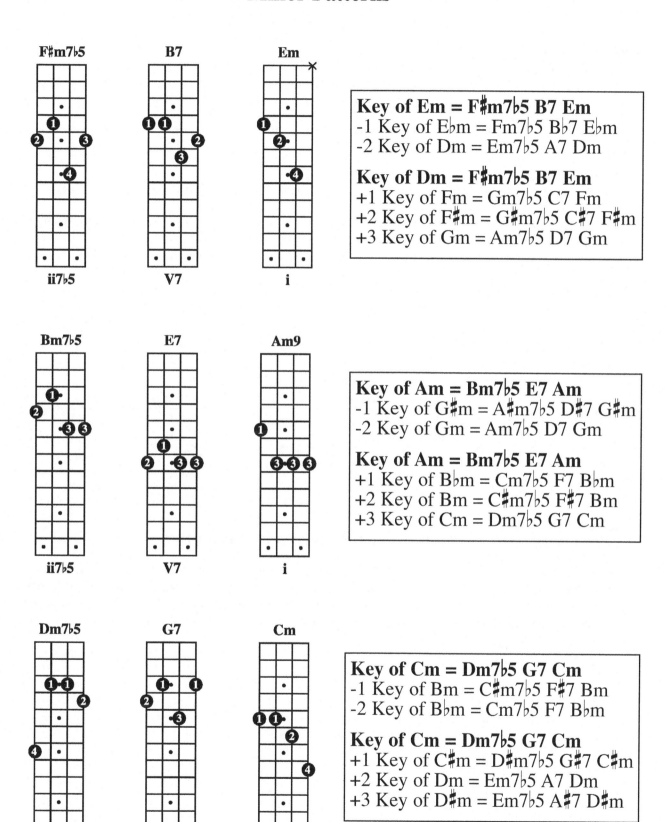

Key of Em = F#m7♭5 B7 Em
-1 Key of E♭m = Fm7♭5 B♭7 E♭m
-2 Key of Dm = Em7♭5 A7 Dm

Key of Dm = F#m7♭5 B7 Em
+1 Key of Fm = Gm7♭5 C7 Fm
+2 Key of F#m = G#m7♭5 C#7 F#m
+3 Key of Gm = Am7♭5 D7 Gm

Key of Am = Bm7♭5 E7 Am
-1 Key of G#m = A#m7♭5 D#7 G#m
-2 Key of Gm = Am7♭5 D7 Gm

Key of Am = Bm7♭5 E7 Am
+1 Key of B♭m = Cm7♭5 F7 B♭m
+2 Key of Bm = C#m7♭5 F#7 Bm
+3 Key of Cm = Dm7♭5 G7 Cm

Key of Cm = Dm7♭5 G7 Cm
-1 Key of Bm = C#m7♭5 F#7 Bm
-2 Key of B♭m = Cm7♭5 F7 B♭m

Key of Cm = Dm7♭5 G7 Cm
+1 Key of C#m = D#m7♭5 G#7 C#m
+2 Key of Dm = Em7♭5 A7 Dm
+3 Key of D#m = Em7♭5 A#7 D#m

How High the Minor Two:
Two Applications of the Exercise

Vertical (Chord)

This takes the classic '**ii V7 I**' progression through all **12 major keys**. Using the first few measures of the popular tune, *"How High the Moon,"* a major chord becomes a minor, and if you work your way backwards from the next two measures, you'll see the way the '**ii V7 I**' cycles through the keys.

This is an excellent opportunity to practice the preceding stock chord patterns in different transpositions and inversions.

Horizontal (Melody)

Here's a chance to take a familiar melody but consciously zero in on scale degree relationships…

Knowing where the **5th, 1st**, and **3rd** scale degrees are will help you effectively define aurally, the tonality of the key when you improvise. Take the time to concentrate on where you are in the scale as you play. You might put the mandolin down, and simply start singing the tune with scale degree names, "**5, 1, 2, 2, 3, 3,**" etc.

Pickup to **Meas. 6**:

Sing the scale degrees in numbers!

When the phrase modulates as in the pickup to measure 6, the two notes begin "**1, 2, 2, 3, 3, 1, 3, 5, 4, 3, 2, 1,**" etc in the new key of **F**. Note when the chord becomes a minor chord (**GMaj7, Gm7; FMaj7, Fm7,** etc), the minor chord is actually preparing for the new key (**Dominant Preparation**). You might wish to go back and review **the preceding Harmonic Function** chapters in this book. This exercise will demonstrate these points quite transparently!

How High the Minor Two

'ii V& I' Study

Major ii V7 I 2nd

To get your fingers to retain tactile memory, practice in 8 measure phrases:

"ii V7" three times, "I" twice!

Pattern begins on 1st scale degree of chord

2nd B♭, B, F, B
FFcP

NO OPEN STRINGS! The concept is to develop **movable**, tactile "home bases" up and down the fretboard. Notice, you can transpose the WHOLE exercise up into the key of F, simply by moving everything over ONE STRING! Transpose to B natural by moving up ONE FRET! Now you have 3 keys. Up a string, up a fret, you have F♯ and 3 of the 12 keys mastered. There will be time for open strings later, but force yourself to learn closed patterns now...

OBSERVE THE BEGINNING NOTE OF EACH PATTERN. With the exception of a couple colorful chromatic passing tones, the exercise intentionally starts with a **specific Chord Tone**, the first, second *(21)* or third *(33)* progressively. Teach your fingers as well as your brain where the **harmonic function** is, and it will free you to improvise between those notes as you develop. (Also it will keep you from ALWAYS starting on a **Chord Root** all the time, a distinguishing mark of less mature players.)

Patterns begins on 3rd scale degree of chord

Patterns begins on 5th scale degree of chord

PLAY AS EIGHT MEASURE PATTERNS. Drill the 'ii V7' into your fingers three times, and give the 7th and 8th measures a time to rest your brain.

PRACTICE AS SWING, AS WELL AS STRAIGHT 8THS. This helps you develop the swing "feel." *(Hint: try using a metronome, but set the clicks for beats 2 and 4.)*

Major ii V7 I 3rd

3rd C, C#, G, A♭
FFcP

Pattern begins on 1st scale degree of chord

MOVABLE SHAPES & RECOGNIZABLE PATTERNS. The purpose of the exercise is to take melodic material you've previously ingested, and start it with another finger position. This is the same melodies, transposed up a step, starting with the 3rd **FFcP.**

MOVE THE EXERCISE UP A FRET. MOVE IT UP A STRING. Your fingers will unconsciously use material, and hopefully vary it later as you add your variations.

BE CONSCIOUS OF SCALE DEGREE FUNCTION. Recognize where the 3rd and 7th scale degree are in relation to the rest of each measure for each chord.

Pattern begins on 3rd scale degree of chord

CONNECT THE NOTES. Play the pattern as a phrase; a long melodic sentence rather than random syllables.

VARY YOUR ACCENTS. Randomize them and make them sound like music, not a drill.

Major ii V7 I 1st

1st Ab, A, Eb, E
FFcP

Pattern begins on 1st scale degree of chord

CHROMATIC DECISIONS. The choice of whether or not to take the downward half-step shift (1st fret) or cross the string (8th fret) is based on the principle that, all things being equal, the first finger affords better power if the 4th finger is heading down an additional 1/2 step. In **Measure 16**, the Eb is better on the 1st fret since the 8th fret shift to the 7th would have less strength.

Lengthening the string (descending) requires more pressure from the finger than going up, so you want the extra "power" available to you from the Eb (1st fret) to D (7th fret).

Ascending is a different story. Shortening the string adds "energy" to the vibration, so a shift upward with the 4th finger is not as difficult.

In **Measure 19**, the D# 8th fret allows better sustain on the 2nd fret E before and after.

Pattern begins on 3rd scale degree of chord

Pattern begins on 5th scale degree of chord

PREPARING FOR UPPER POSITIONS. The goal is to be able to take the security and comfort of these patterns up into higher frets. For academic purposes, we're keeping the exercise on only three strings, so the suggested fingering in **Measure 39** is not only preparing you for when you play them in the keys of E♭ and E, but to begin thinking about crossing positions, and taking the rest of the exercises into the upper frets.

Major ii V7 I 4th

4th Db, D, Ab, A
FFcP

Pattern begins on 1st scale degree of chord

4th FINGER POSITION: Because the fingering starts so high, there are some suggested fingerings which facilitate a smoother shift from a lower position on the fingerboard to the higher positions. Practice the "shifts" isolating the last note prior to the shift and the first note after. Set your fingers and let your hands and wrists get familiar with what it feels like to move from one "stance" to the next. Move as quickly and as smoothly as possible, hardly lifting the fingers off the strings at all.

CONSIDER THE POWER OF THE ASCENDING. Chromatic shifts upward are always easier, as vibration energy is not lost when you shorten the string. Conversely, you need extra effort and fingertip grip to maintain vibration on a downward shift on the same string.

69

Pattern begins on 3rd scale degree of chord

LEARNING THE 4th FFcP LAST. Because this one is that hardest, make sure you are comfortable with the first three before spending much time on this. You won't use this as much, but there is still great benefit in mastering it.

70

Minor ii7♭5 V7 i

1st FFcP
G♯, A, D♯, E

Pattern begins on 1st scale degree of chord

RICH HARMONIC OPPORTUNITIES IN MINOR. Too much time can be spent drilling the different forms of the harmonic, natural, and melodic minor scales. In jazz, it's more important to understand and isolate the context of the dominant chord, and how it functions in resolving to the tonic.

Learn these variations, but rest assured that you are given much liberty in which form to use. Above all, use your ear.

(Ear first, Theory second!!)

Pattern begins on 3rd scale degree of chord

Pattern begins on 5th scale degree of chord

ALTERED SCALE. Much more is possible with the Altered Scale, but Measure 28 gives you a little taste of what can be done…

Minor ii7♭5 V7 i

2nd B♭, B, F, E♯
FFcP

Pattern begins on 1st scale degree of chord

REVIEW: Chromatic shifts up 1/2 step shorten the string and increase the "energy" of the vibration, so you can get away without starting the sound of the 2nd note with another finger (**Measure 18**, 4th beat to **Measure 19**, 1st beat.)

Pattern begins on 3rd scale degree of chord

ALTERED SCALE. Used in **Measure 28**.

REVIEW: Chromatic shifts downward lose energy (vibration) so it is best to hit **Measure 32**, 3rd beat with a new finger (rather than slide).

Minor ii7♭5 V7 i

3rd C, C♯, F, F♯
FFcP

Pattern begins on 1st scale degree of chord

CHECKING OUT THE OTHER KEYS: Hopefully, by now you've tried the other patterns in the exercise by moving them up a fret and/or string. Eventually, these will be second nature to your fingers. Notice in the top left hand corner of each FFcP, the suggested listing of other keys that work quite smoothly with the fingering.

USING THE EXERCISES IN CONTEXT: Take the time to explore songs you know and see how these patterns might fit.

Pattern begins on 3rd scale degree of chord

Pattern begins on 5th scale degree of chord

POSITION SHIFT: Remember the shift up the fingerboard in **Measure 39** is merely academic at this point. In the "real world" you would play the C minor pattern on the 1st string, but for now, experiment with the upper frets, as written.

76

Minor ii7♭5 V7 i

4th D, C♯, A, G♯
FFcP

Pattern begins on 1st scale degree of chord

4th FFcP: As in the Major Patterns, the **4th FFcP** isn't quite as practical, but you will use it much more when you play in the upper frets. Take the opportunity to learn the finger scale degree *relationships* in the more familiar terrain of the lower frets.

HALF STEPS: Slides or chromatic shifts by one fret will sound slightly weaker on the second note. When possible, make the shift on the upbeat and save the string crossing for a downbeat, as in **Measure 34** (first beat). **Measure 37** (fourth beat) shows the converse-start beat 4 on the 3rd (new finger) for a stronger sound.

Blues 501: Advanced Blues Progressions

The uniquely American art of **Blues** music has almost evolved into a "universal" language of its own. In the century since its roots in the North American continent, the simple **12 bar pattern** has been adopted and adapted by jazz musicians, and infused with a more sophisticated set of changes and harmonic complexity.

Earlier Blues...

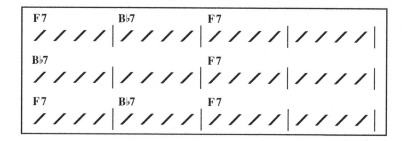

In its most primitive, raw form, three chords suffice to cover the blues. In the above changes, you only need the **I, IV, and V** chords, with the signature alteration of a **lowered 7th**, or a dominant functioning chord. What's unique, is unlike the rest of Western (European) music, this dominant doesn't ever resolve to a pure form of **tonic** (or **I**). To our ears accustomed to the blues, it offers its own kind of unique stability.

Jazzers participate in a **hybrid** form of the blues, blending its own vocabulary of '**ii V7**' motion with the raw skeletal structure. The result, along with about a half dozen common conventions or alterations, yields a fresh approach to this passionate music. We want to take a closer look at some of the possibilities.

Blues 501

Chick'n Apple Scrapple

Ted Eschliman

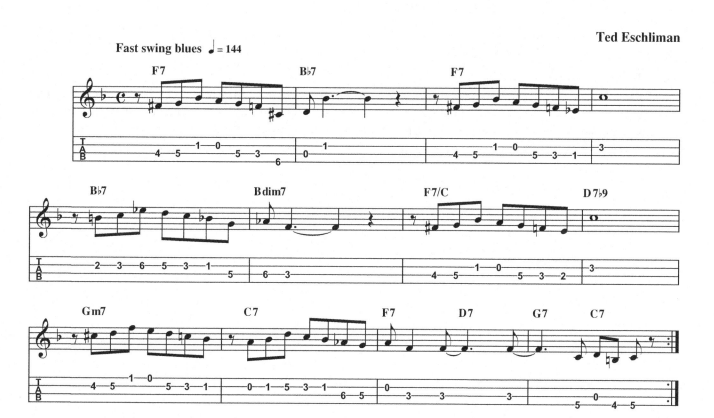

79

The tune *"Chick'n Apple Scrapple"* borrows from a few of the more advanced variations of the "pure" blues form. Notice the substitution of the **Bdim7** in meas. 6 and the **D7♭9** in **meas. 8**. This breaks up the stagnancy, and with the **D7♭9**, we have a kind of **"Secondary Dominant"** (dominant of the ii7!) in that the stripped down 'D7' chord is the 'V7' of the **Gm7** chord in **meas. 9** which, incidentally, is the **ii7** in our home key of '**F**.'

The last two measures tour us through another round of **"Secondary Dominants"** or **"Circle of Fifths."** Commonly known as **"Turnarounds,"** the two-measure variations on what would have been just the tonic chord (or even an added **V7**) breathe a whole new life into the end of a chorus. There are more variations on this that you'll need to add to your line card, but we'll save the "**Turnaround**" concept for later. Let's look at some other opportunities for fresh blues structure:

Basic Jazz
Blues

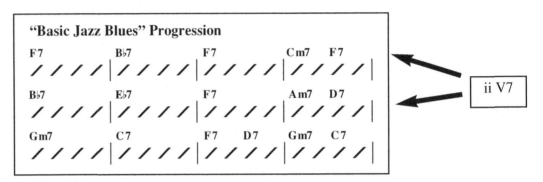

The first substitution we'll look at is in **m. 4**, the **Cm7 F7** chords. Using your astute music analysis skills, you've probably noticed the temporary shift in tonal center to the key of B♭ in **meas. 5**. If you're really on the ball, you noted that the **Cm7 & F7** measures form a '**ii V7**' preparation for these measures. Already we're expanding the stagnancy of one chord to a whole preliminary "sentence" prepping for the key of **B♭**.

Looking at **meas. 8**, it's the same addition of a '**ii V7**,' the **Am7 D7** introducing a **Gm7** chord. Even though it may be questionable if the **Gm7** is actually a new key, the sense of tonality doesn't exist long enough to be an issue, as the **Gm7** morphs back into the '**ii7**' chord of F. (Note: you can inject this '**ii V7**' alteration in myriads other situations for a pleasant sense of motion.)

Finally, we see another kind of "Turnaround" in the last two measures, a simple '**ii V7**' bringing us back to home key, preceded by the **V7** (D7) of the **Gm7**. We'll explore turnarounds in more detail, later.

Introducing Harmonic Function

As you may have just noticed, the Blues are an unintimidating way of introducing **Harmonic Function**. Unencumbered by complex key modulations, you see plenty of opportunity to vary a static, stark 12 bar form. Simply injecting a few '**ii V7**' chords, or even a **Secondary Dominant** (**V7** of any chord based on the scale), you've enriched the music. You can apply this kind of variation (and will!) in almost any music.

More Blues Alterations

"Swing" blues á la Jethro Burns (although he certainly wasn't the first!) introduces some more tasty changes to the diatonic (major) scale.

Swing Jazz Blues

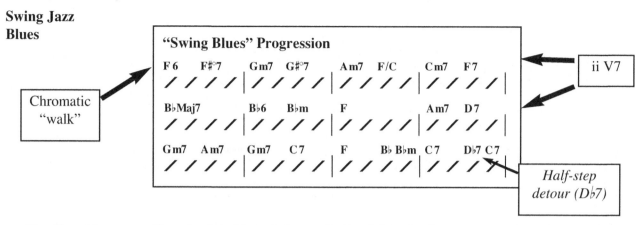

The first thing you will notice is a kind of chromatic "walk" in the first two measures. If you took the first chord (only) of each measure, you have a "diatonic" walk that uses the **F Major Scale, F, Gm7 Am7**. But inserting the diminished chords on the third beat (**F#°7, G#°7**) gives you some "motion" to the progression, leading you to a '**ii V7**' set-up for the (temporary) key of Bb in **m. 5.**

The **minor iv** or **Bbm** in **meas. 6** is a nice spice we can add, and of course we have the same "prep" progression in **meas. 8**, as the **Am7 D7** chords set up the **Gm7** in **meas. 9**. The **Am7** is a sort of diatonic "drift," followed by the home key '**ii V7**' in **meas. 10**.

The "**Turnaround**" final two measures is yet another approach to adding variety and returning us to the home key of **F**. The last measure is mainly the **C7** chord with a half step "detour" **Db7**. Later we'll talk about **Tri-tone substitutions** (the **Db7** could also be replaced by **G7**, and have the same role in spicing up the **C7** chord).

Bebop Jazz Blues

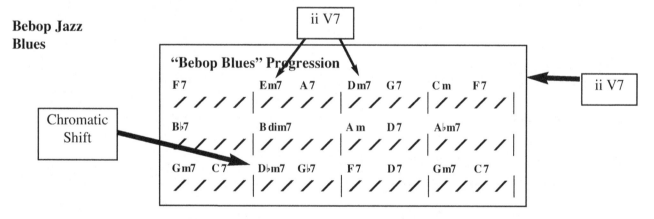

The Bebop Era wrought its own sophisticated chord mutations. If you are familiar with the '**ii V7**' relationship, you will see the concept explode here. The "set-up of the set-up" the "preparation of the preparation," you'll observe that we've extended the **4th measure**. **Cm/F7** by inserting a **Dm7/G7** in the previous measure. This is the '**ii V7**' of the **Cm** chord! Go backwards to the second measure, and it's the same relationship, the **Em7/A7** is the '**ii V7**' of the **Dm7** chord.

In **meas. 10**, we do something different with a '**ii V7**;' the **G♭7** is a half-step higher than the tonic **F7** in the **11th measure**, and it is "prepared" by its '**ii**' the **D♭m7**. This is an even more complex twist to the "half step detour" we witnessed in the Swing Blues.

"Bird" Blues

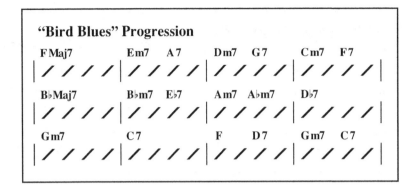

This is a common variation, Charlie Parker "signature" blues. It doesn't vary that much from the *Bebop Blues,"* except for the **Maj7** in the **1st** and **5th measures**. Substituting the **Fmaj7** for the **F7** departs from the characteristic blues restlessness, even though we stay within the basic 12 bar blues framework.

Turnarounds

We want to explore variations on the last two measures of the advanced blues patterns. These can be substituted at will, depending on what the other rhythm players are doing. The essence of these two bars is a cycle of fifths; sometimes the V of V (and its preceding chord) could be either **major** or **minor**.

Another substitution is a chromatic descending chord which is also a **tri-tone substitution**.

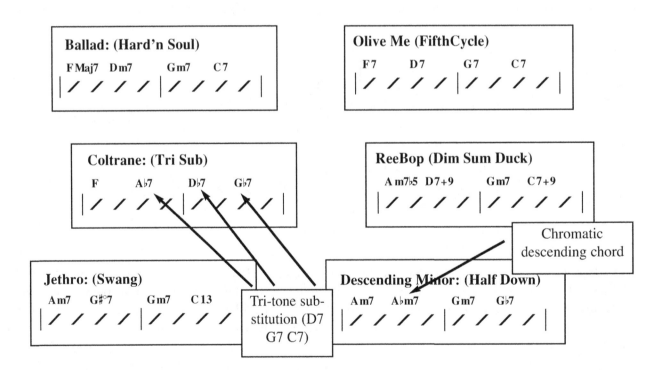

We'll look at some melodic **Turnaround Patterns** more closely later in the book.

Minor Blues

The topic of the Blues would hardly be complete without looking at a few Minor Blues options. These can also offer a delicious variety of harmonic progression; however, the complexity still won't betray the underlying Dominant Prep/Dominant functions throughout. You'll find some interesting detours, certainly, but you don't stray much from the 12 bar sense of "home," away, and back home again.

Minor Blues Progression (Basic)

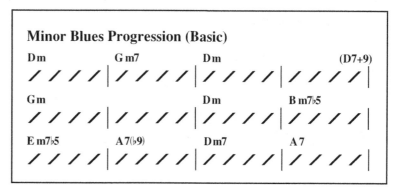

Not much surprise here; other than the m7♭5 characteristic of a 'ii' chord and some liberties with V7 extensions we haven't changed much from the Major Blues.

Alternate Minor Blues Progression

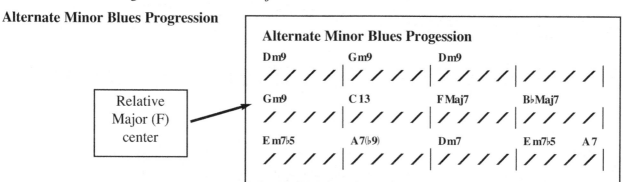

This journeys into the Relative Major Key (F Major). It's a refreshing detour; ultimately though, we are back to the minor key, or at least setting it up in the final measure.

Modal (Minor) Blues Progression

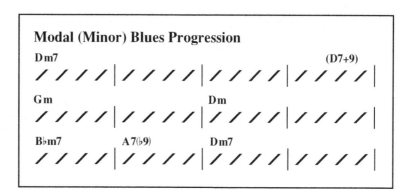

Notice a 'retreat' to simplicity inherent in the Modal Blues. As a reaction to the later Bebop era, musicians such as trumpeter Miles Davis abandoned the typically fast past harmonic changes in exchange for structural simplicity. Though they would slow the progression down, a new artform of implying 'subchanges' within the change allowed a soloist more freedom to play in and out of the changes. (You can still inject 'Turnaround' patterns at will, and are expected to make it interesting in this way as an improviser...)

Chick'n Apple Scrapple
(501 Blues Example)

Ted Eschliman

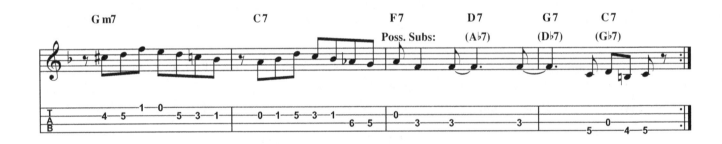

Turn Around Progressions
(Key of F)

FMaj7 **Dm7** **Gm7** (9) **C7**

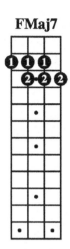 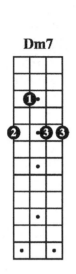 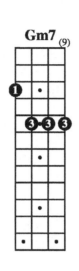 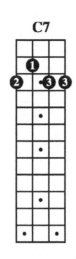

Ballad...

The most basic two measure **Turnaround** is a familiar 'I **iv7 ii7 V7**' that doesn't break the confines of the diatonic scale. Because of this, this popular 'Doo Wop' progression is very easy to improvise over; you stay within the original key center. With no chromatic alterations, this 'vanilla' combination limits the tension to the subtle but final pull of the **leading tone** (7) and **4th** scale degree to the **tonic** and **3rd** scale degree (E to F, B♭ to A).

F7 **D7** **G7** **C7**

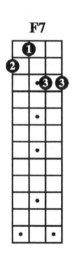 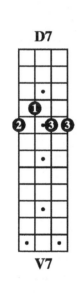 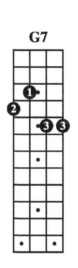 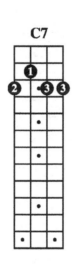

V7

Olive Me...

The two chords outside of the **key center** (**F**) are **D7** and **G7**. In retrospect, these **Secondary Dominant** chords precede each other as a '**V7 of V7**,' where **D7** is the **V of G7**, which is the **V of C7**. You'll hear this commonly referred to as the **Circle of Fifths**.

FMaj7 **A♭7** **D♭7** **G♭7**

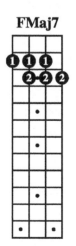 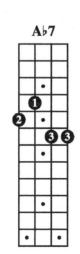 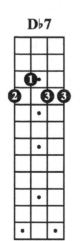 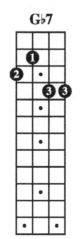

Coltrane...

Similar to its predecessor in its **Secondary Dominant** functions, we inject a very subtle twist; The '**D7 G7 C7**' are swapped, or substituted by its **Tri-tone substitution,** '**A♭7 D♭7 G♭7.**' Note that these chords share the compelling 'Tri-tone' pull notes. See this mapped out in the **Two Note Chord Variation**.

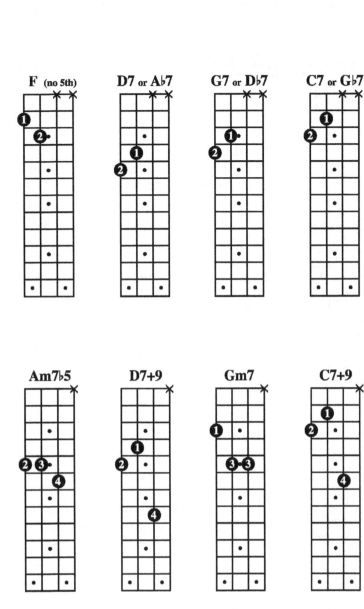

F (no 5th)   D7 or A♭7   G7 or D♭7   C7 or G♭7

Two Note Chord…
(a.k.a. "Guide Tones")

We can isolate the **3rd** and **7th** of these chords. Boiled to its essence, these are the "meat" tones of the chords. Observe they descend by half steps, or by one fret; this is a consistent pattern or "trick" you can exploit whenever you recognize a sequence of multiple **Secondary Dominants**, or **Circle of Fifths**.

Am7♭5   D7+9   Gm7   C7+9

Reebop…

Note the introduction of +9 extension. Also, whether the third chord is **Gm7** or **G7** is moot at fast tempos. *(The B natural can be the leading tone of the C chord…)*

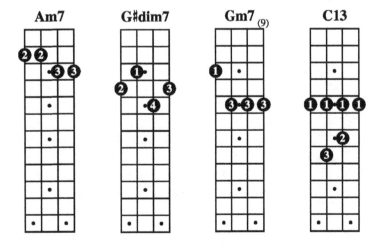

Am7   G♯dim7   Gm7 (9)   C13

Jethro…

Again, we've added some richer extensions. A **diminished chord** always wants to pull toward a more stable chord. Note the **Gm7** is really a **Gm9**, this is fine as long as the other ensemble members aren't introducing a conflicting +9 or ♭9.

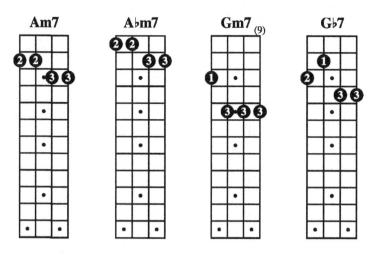

Am7   A♭m7   Gm7 (9)   G♭7

Descending Minor...

Sometimes a simple **1/2 step descension** or **ascension** can bring out a strong sense of motion. Note the **tri-tone sub** of **G♭7** for **C7** the last measure. It also has the same half step pull as **E** (**F♭**) and **B♭** that resolve respectively to **F** and **A.**

Understanding the principles and purpose of the **turnaround** gives you fabulous opportunity to freshen the most basic (and static!) of patterns. Even when it's not obvious in the chording of the accompanying ensemble, you still have the option of introducing these "flavors" in your soloing melodically.

Chord Voicing

The patterns we've laid out are intended to start you using your own voicings in other keys. You'll want to begin unraveling your own, whether digging them out of a chord dictionary, or if experienced enough in music theory, creating your own.

Important principles for creating your own variations:

1.) **Resolve your "leading tones."** Avoid awkward leaps from your "gravity notes" (**3rd, 7th, ♭9th**) as they only need to move a half step or pull one fret over. Don't skip all over the fretboard.

2.) **Minimize the movement of each of your own chord variations from one to the next.** Try to keep the basic block from moving more than three frets if possible. If you find you have to move farther, it's time to find another way to finger it!

As you develop your own chord vocabulary these will become an almost subconscious or subliminal process. The more you play, the more "background thinking" these will become.

These are a good start, though!

Mandolin Chord User Template

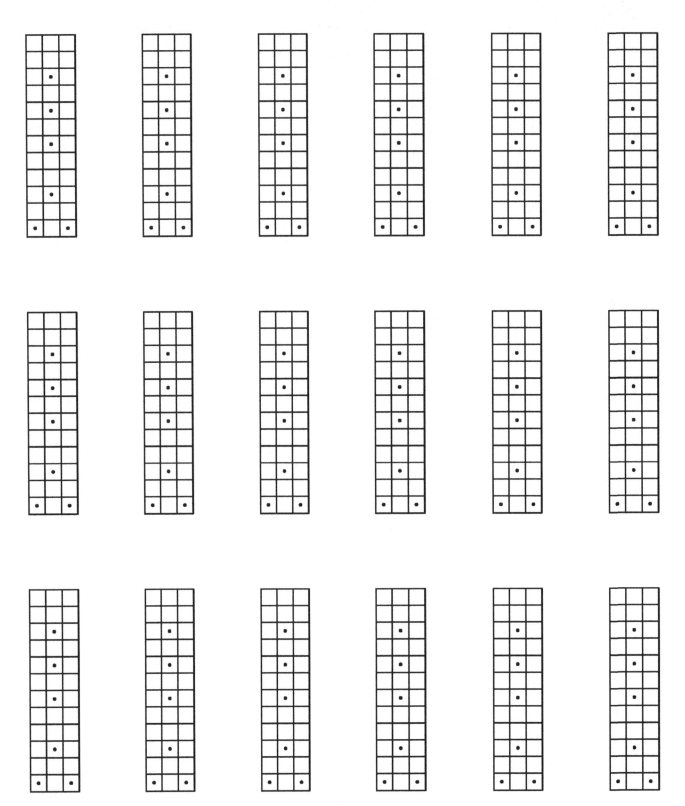

Hint: Make copies of this page for your own set of blanks.
www.jazzmando.com

Turnarounds

Track #33

3rd G, A♭, C, C#
FFcP

Patterns to "re-cycle" back to tonic

Note: Accents are merely academic. The point is to identify the "guide" tones of the 3rd & 7th of each chord.

Above accented notes are the "guide" tones–the 3rd & 7th of each chord.

2nd FFcP
F, F♯, B♭, B

Above accented notes are the "guide" tones–the 3rd & 7th of each chord.

1st FFcP
Eb, E, A, Ab

Above accented notes are the "guide" tones–the 3rd & 7th of each chord.

91

4th A, A♭, D, D♭

FFcP

Above accented notes are the "guide" tones–the 3rd & 7th of each chord.

Tri-tone Substitutions

Tri-tone Sub

You've probably heard the term **Tri-tone** before. It's a powerful scale degree relationship that fuels the energy within Western (European) music. Arguably one of the most dissonant intervals, it's the "meat" of the **Dominant** functioning cord, the sound that longs for resolution to a **Tonic** chord.

The **Tri-tone** is two notes; think of it as six frets apart, three whole steps, or music theory buffs will label it a **Diminished 5th** or **Augmented 4th** (same), depending on the context (where it will resolve). This mysterious sounding combination is a ripe sound in and of itself, but digging deeper into harmonic analysis, it gives us fertile ground for terrific opportunities to expand beyond diatonic conventions without being abandoned in chromatic oblivion. *It's the music/mathematical equivalent of formula $A^2 + B^2 = C^2$!*

Take a **Bb7** chord, **Bb, D, F, Ab**. The magic of this **Dominant** 7th chord lies in the **D** and **Ab** relationship. As we mentioned before, you could strip away the **F**, even omit the root **Bb** and you'd have a powerful dominant functioning sound. In the key of **Eb**, where **Bb7** is the **V7**, the **Tri-tone** interval seeks resolutions to the **1st** and **3rd** of the key, the **Eb** and **G:**

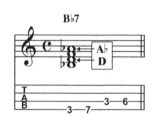

| D to Eb |
| Ab to G |

But wait, there's more! The **D** can move a **1/2 step** in the opposite direction from **D** to **C#**, and the enharmonic **G#** (**Ab**!) could resolve to an **A:**

| Ab = G# |

| D to C# |
| G# tp A |

These are the "guts" of an **E7** chord, which is the **V7 in the key of A**. Note the relationship of the **key of A** to the key **Eb**... You guessed it, a **Tri-tone!**

This demonstrates the opportunity for fresh harmonic journeys in what jazzers call **"Tri-tone Substitution."** Knowing these relationships help, and there are only six of them!

Note the second set of relationships is identical; you merely swap left for right.

A7	Eb7	Eb7	A7
Bb7	E7	E7	Bb7
B7	F7	F7	B7
C7	Gb7	Gb7	C7
Db7 (C#7)	G7	G7	Db7 (C#7)
D7	Ab7 (G#7)	Ab7 (G#7)	D7

Tri-tone Sub Applications

1.) Replace any **V7** chord with its Tri-tone equivalent. The previous example was **Bb7** or **V7 chord in the key of Eb**. We replaced this with an **E7**, which is the lowered two chord (**bII7**), and coincidentally, **1/2 step up** from the **Tonic** (D).

2.) Break up a stagnant diatonic "**Turnaround**" succession. Referring back to the earlier topic of "**Turnarounds**," we took the stock "vanilla" progression F7, **Dm7, Gm7, C7** (I7, vi7, ii7, V7) and raised the **3rds** to get a progression of dominants. We end up with F7, **D7, G7, C7**, and now modify the last 3 chords with F7, **Ab7, Db7, Gb7**. (If you take the time to look at the **Tri-tone** "guts" of each of the last 3 chords of the second Turnaround, you have the same enharmonic notes.)

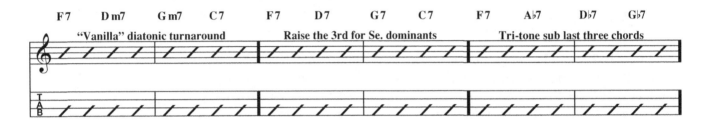

3.) Mix them up. The previous **F7, D7, G7, C7** turnaround could be **F7, D7, Db7, C7**, as well.

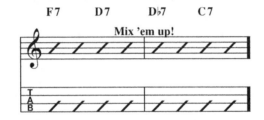

4.) Use the scales of the **Tri-tone substitution** even if the other players aren't "subbing." This gives you an "outside" flavor that comes back to tonic nicely; if you were playing a string of secondary dominants '**I, VI7, II7, V7**' in F, it would be **F, D7, G7, C7**, you could inject soloing extracted from a the chords of **Ab7 for the D7, Db7 for the G7** chord, and **Gb7 for the C7** chord. Keep in mind you'd be playing major scale with a lowered 7th degree (commonly called a **Mixolydian** scale) based on the root of the **Tri-tone sub**.

Melodic Tri-tone substituting

Mandolin Chord Economics

If you're at the level where you have enough theory under your belt and you've thrown away your chord dictionary, or even if you just want to improve the way you finger certain chord voicings, the subject of chord "economics" is significant, especially for the rich extensions unearthed in jazz...

Besides the mandolin, there are very few musical instruments outside of ukulele and tenor banjo that have only four strings to accompany or "comp." This is usually no problem in the more diatonic folk genres, when the only expectations in chordal harmony are **root, 3rd, 5th**, and the occasional **7th**. It is only with the unique extensions of **9th, 11th, and 13th** of jazz that you end up with more voices than strings.

A unique dilemma...
Six voices, four strings.

Take the chord **B♭13(♭9)** for example. You have the following voices to express.

B♭, D, F, A♭, C♭, G,

It is only in the "extended" harmonic vocabulary of jazz you end up with more voices than strings...

B♭	root
D	3rd
F	5th
A♭	(implied in all 13th chords) 7th
C♭	9th
G	13th
Six voices, Four Strings	

The **13th** of the chord is like the **6th** (you already knew that) but the **13th** always implies adding the **7th** (the A♭). It IS part of the chord. Otherwise, it would be called a "**6**" chord (**B♭6**).

Now if you want to get technical, you can voice it by keeping the meaty **tri-tone** relationship (**D & A♭**) of the **3rd & 7th** in the lower strings (always good), voicing the **13th** and the **♭9** on your E and A string, and get ready for some fret gymnastics:

D=3, A♭=7, G=13, C♭=(♭9)

But wait; OUCH!...

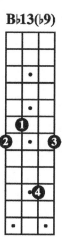

B♭13(♭9)

Not only is this hard to play, it even sounds horrible out of context. Now, you might actually use this, but let's suggest a more "real world" approach would be to break it up into **B♭13**, and **B♭(♭9)** chords, and divide it up over time.

This is an example where music theory and sensibility clash, and you have license to voice only a part of the chord at a time...

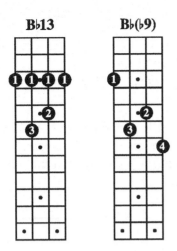

Bb13   Bb(b9)

The reason to use these fingerings: when you **voice the lower strings** this way, it gives you the flexibility of moving your pinky in an out of both positions quite easily. Then you can "imply" the harmonic structure by playing it again in the same harmonic context.

This is why we call it "**economics**;" it's simply unrealistic to expect to be able to always apply the full extensions guitar (let alone piano) players are able to voice. You have to use a little ingenuity!

You could go back to the first voicing and drop the **3rd** finger, or just mute the E string. Much of this will depend on context, but knowing some basic principles well help you make decisions for yourself on what to use.

Chord Voice Priorities

1.) The **3rd** and the **7th** are the most important voices! It's best when you can voice them in your lowest two strings (more acoustically fundamental).

2.) You don't have to voice the I or **tonic** if you're playing with an instrument lower in pitch. They will, and you don't need to duplicate it.

3.) The **5th**, unless it's a flat or augmented five doesn't have to be played. Acoustically implied, it's a "benign" tone that doesn't have much power or pull.

4.) Any fingers left over can handle the extensions, the **9th**, **11th**, **13th**. Best if these are in the highest strings, and that's why we want them handled by the pinky whenever possible.

| Tonic or Root (Someone else's job!) |
| **Third: Majorness/Minorness** |
| Fifth (always implied except when diminished or augmented) |
| **Seventh: Stability resolved or "to be" resolved** |
| Color (Extensions **9th**, **11th**, **13th**, sus) |

....

This doesn't have to be an intimidating thought process. You don't have to include all the notes of a **six-note chord**. You can ignore the lower priority notes, leave some of the color to the other players, or get the different voices over a couple strums of the chord.

Knowing these principles should FREE you for some tasty harmonic flavors! This is where the mandolin really shines!

G♭13-9 "Chop"?

Mandolin Chord User Template

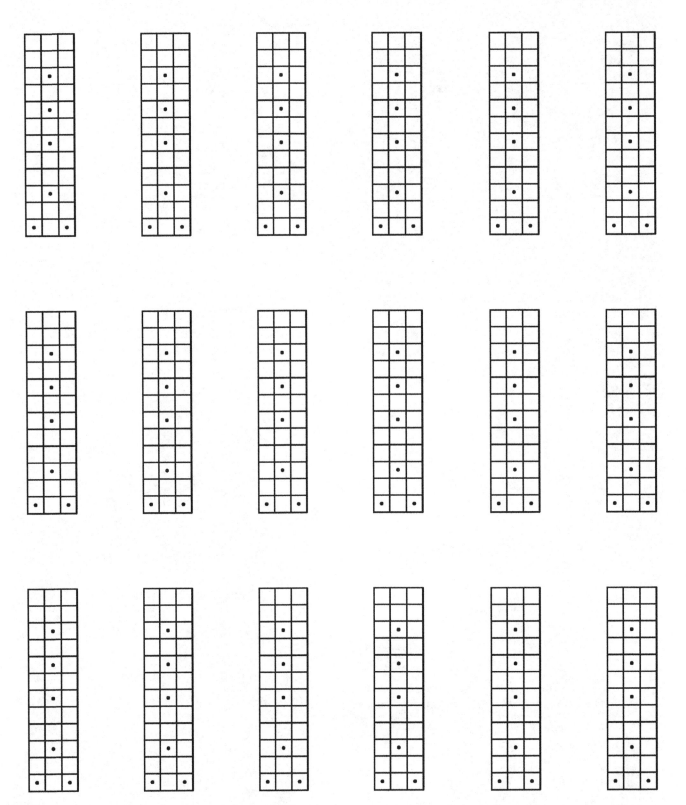

Symmetrical Fretboard "Tricks"
Diminished and Augmented Chords

The **Perfect 5th** (GDAE) tuning affords us some lovely alternatives on the mandolin fingerboard! Exploring the "symmetrical" **triad** and **7th chord** options yields a fascinating geometric shape on the frets that makes some interesting tactile patterns you will find on few other instruments.

Major, Minor, Diminished, Augmented

You are familiar with **Major** and **Minor triads**. The **5th** is the same, but the **3rd** is either an interval of **3 frets** (half steps) or **4**. (The distance between the **3rd** and **5th** gives you another interval of a **3rd**.) Let's explore the two other triad possibilities, **Diminished**, and **Augmented.**

"Symmetrical" Chords

The **Diminished** triad and **Augmented**, stack two equal distant **3rds** on top of each other, the **Diminished** is two **Minor 3rds**, the Augmented is two **Major 3rds**. Extend the Diminished triad by another **minor 3rd** and you have a **Diminished 7th** chord.

Adim7

A♭ Aug

Adim is **A, C, E♭**
Adim7 is **A, C, E♭, G♭, (F♯)**
Here we have an inversion to fit the fingers, **A, E♭, C, G♭**

A♭ Augmented is **A♭, C, E**, (start again with **A♭**)
Here we have an inversion to fit the fingers, **A♭, E, C, A♭**

Notice because the mandolin is tuned in equal 5ths, we see recurring "diagonal" shapes to the chords, like birds flying south for the winter *(if you live north of the Equator...)*.

You can stick with a **triad** (3 notes) spelling, don't feel compelled to always use all four strings. (You can even use a powerful two note chord in diminished; the inherent tri-tone (**A & E♭**) stands on its own as a sonic energy builder.)

The **Diminished 7th** chord is rich with tension; notice the 7th chord includes TWO tri-tone intervals, **A & E♭, C & G♭**. Again, you don't need to play all four notes. You'll find this concept useful in playing **7(♭9)** chords in that in essence the **7(♭9)** is basically a rootless diminished chord. In the above Adim7, you have a rootless **F7(♭9)** chord:

F, A, C, E♭, G♭. Leave out the **F** and you have an **Adim7**!

The **Augmented** chord was used frequently in Swing, a personal favorite of Jethro Burns. As a **Dominant Functioning** chord, the raised **5th** likes to resolve upward to the color **3rd** of the home (Tonic) key. **A♭, C, E** as a (A♭ Aug) **Dominant** in **D♭ Major** would have the E resolve comfortably to an F which is the 3rd of the tonal center.

What's fun with the symmetrical aspects of these chords is how they repeat themselves in other keys.

Diminished 7ths

See the visual pattern! Notice, each shape is the same notes, but starts with a different root. Instead of learning 12 different diminished chords then, there are only 3, before it starts to repeat itself again. Plus, you have the option of voicing your chords conveniently to the next ones they resolve to.

Adim7

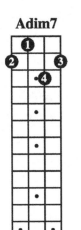

Cdim7

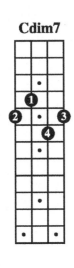

E♭dim7

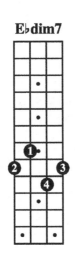

F♯dim7

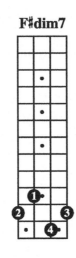

Augmented

The symmetry is even more striking here. Note, it's even less necessary to play all four notes of the chord, since you are duplicating pitches. Still, this can be a very spicy addition to a changes; it can be as simple as **raising the 5th** of any **Dominant Functioning** chord. Instead of 12 chords, you have 4 sets before the chord starts to repeat itself again (with a different root).

A♭ Aug

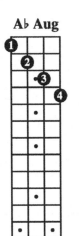

C Aug

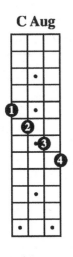

E Aug

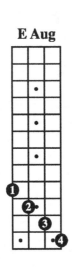

Dominate!

These are fabulous options for any **Dominant Functioning** chord. More importantly they can free you very quickly from being trapped in the lower frets. Again, don't feel the need to play all four strings. Even the **Tritone**, two-note chord is a powerful enough sound without the extra notes.

Beyond Tonal Centers

The Tonal Universe

Understanding the "**Tonal Universe**" concept, the relationship of tonic, dominant, and dominant preparation (**ii, V7, I**) hands you the keys to the driving force of jazz literature throughout the majority of the 20th century. It's the **Tonal Center** that outlines a single scale, major or minor, in which you can improvise freely and intelligently through these measures. Knowing where you are, and more importantly, where you'll end up gives your improvisation the direction and focus of a well-crafted solo!

The **Tonal Centers** can be whole sections of music, or as brief as a half measure. Songs can be comprised of a few well-connected keys, or a delicious set of contrasting, detouring changes. Take the time to isolate these centers in your music, whether mentally or going as far as **penciling them into your music** (not a bad idea for the jazz novice).

As a general rule, the earlier the jazz music was written, the less complicated these tonal centers are. As jazz progressed from the early 20th century in a simple blues, to a '**Circle of 5ths**' Dixieland, to lush Broadway song adaptations, these relationships evolved into more complex and profoundly more ambiguous chord changes.

The lightning fast changes of the 50's & 60's Bebop Era increased the speed of these changes. The later 20th century introduced polytonalities and the "Third Stream" vocabularies of atonality.

As a simple folk mandolinist, you may have found it a challenge just getting out of the key of "G." Don't let these later forms of jazz intimidate you, though. **Ambiguity begets license**; when the harmony is more obscure and less defined, you really aren't as trapped by the conventions of Western (European) Music **tension** and **resolution**. This is not an excuse to never learn the "rules," but it does free you up to evolve in them as you get better.

We're going to leave you with a song that moves the tonal centers faster. Notice you can have an entirely different key in each measure, but this eventually settles down later in the song. The first page is the song itself, the second, a harmonic analysis or tonal center "map."

Do this with your own favorite songs. If you're reading standard notation, look for accidentals (♯'s or ♭'s). Unless these are brief chromatic passing tones, they are the clue to a tonal center change. Find the **V7** (or diminished) chord and see where it lands. This is probably your new key.

Finally, listen for moments of relative stability and resolution, and analyze backwards. Setting them up will be your **Dominant** functioning chord, and likely **Preparation** chords preceding that. You'll get to the point where you see the bigger picture '**ii V7 I**' cells just like you intuitively recognize whole sentences in written language.

Listen for moments of relative stability and resolution, and analyze *backwards*.

Yes, I'll Always Be There

Ted Eschliman

Yes, I'll Always Be There

Ted Eschliman

Jazz Waltz ♩ = 112

System 1

| C Maj7 | B♭ Maj7 | A Maj7 | C Maj7 | F Maj7 | B♭ Maj7 |

3/4

| I: Key of C Maj | I: Key of B♭ Maj | I: Key of A Maj | I: Key of C Maj | IV: Key of C Maj | I: Key of B♭ Maj |
| C Maj Scale | B♭ Maj Scale | A Maj Scale | C Maj Scale | ∕. | B♭ Maj Scale |

System 2

| E♭ Maj7 | F Maj7 | D Maj7 | | D m Dm(Maj7) D m7 | G 9 |

| I: Key of B♭ Maj | I: Key of F Maj | I: Key of D Maj | | ii: Key of C Maj | V7: Key of C Maj |
| ∕. | F Maj Scale | D Maj Scale | ∕. | C Maj Scale | ∕. |

System 3

| C Maj7 | F Maj7 | F m7 | B♭7 | E♭ Maj7 | D m7 G 9 |

| I: Key of C Maj | IV: Key of C Maj | ii: Key of E♭ Maj | V7: Key of E♭ Maj | I: Key of E♭ Maj | ii & V7: Key of C Maj |
| ∕. | ∕. | B♭ Maj Scale | ∕. | ∕. | C Maj Scale |

System 4

| C Maj7 | F Maj7 | C Maj7 | F Maj7 | E m7 ('ii V7' of ii) | A 7(♭9) |

| I: Key of C Maj | IV: Key of C Maj | I: Key of C Maj | IV: Key of C Maj | ii: Key of D Maj | V7: Key of D Maj |
| ∕. | ∕. | ∕. | ∕. | D Maj Scale | (A Alt Scale) |

System 5

| D m7 | B♭13 | C Maj7 | F Maj7 | C Maj7 | F Maj7 | E m7 ('ii V7' of ii) |

| i: Key of Dm | V7: Key of E♭ Maj | I: Key of C Maj | IV: Key of C Maj | I: Key of C Maj | IV: Key of C Maj | ii: Key of D Maj |
| C Maj Scale | B♭ Maj Scale | C Maj Scale | ∕. | ∕. | ∕. | D Maj Scale |

System 6

| A 7 | D m7 | B♭9 | C Maj7 | B♭ Maj7 | A 7 (V7 of ii) |

| V7: Key of D Maj | i: Key of Dm | ♭VII7: Key of C Maj | I: Key of C Maj | I: Key of B♭ Maj | V7: Key of Dm |
| ∕. | C Maj Scale | E♭ Maj Scale | C Maj Scale | B♭ Maj Scale | D Maj Scale |

System 7

| A aug7 | D m7 | 1. | Last X only G 9 | C Maj7 | A♭7(♯11) | C Maj7 |

| V7: Key of Dm | ii: Key of C Maj | | V7: Key of C Maj | I: Key of C Maj | V7: Key of D♭ Maj | I: Key of C Maj |
| (A Alt Scale) | C Maj Scale | ∕. | ∕. | ∕. | D♭ Maj Scale | C Maj Scale |

103

Improvisation:
Pattern Based vs. Theory Based

Let's take a moment to explore the skill of creating music on the spot; the art of **improvising**. The idea of wasting hours of time learning the clinical structure in the academic "laboratory" of music theory, and never taking it to the next step by using it in the real world may seem disheartening. An approach in our charter is to always apply the application alongside the "rule." Talk until you're blue in the face about principles of music, but context always trumps principle! It always boils down to the ear and what intuitively sounds good.

The best way to approach developing improvisational skills is to think of it in two equally (but inseparable) strategies. **Pattern Based**, where the music thought, motif, phrase is already stated or created, and **Theory Based**, where rule or better, "convention" dictates what notes are fertile for generating music.

Theory Based (Conventions):

Advantages:
Fewer notes which exploit musical meaning through tension/resolution
Quicker access to "appropriate" melodic material
Elimination of not only wrong notes, but modal meandering

Disadvantages:
Sterile and clinical, not prone to creativity by itself
Cerebral, artistically dispassionate
Less prone to the intrinsic beauty of "chance"

Pattern Based (Riffs):

Advantages:
Immediate and accessible melodic material
Readily tactile and easily transported to other keys
Musically complete "thought" in short context

Disadvantages:
Limiting when not "metamorphasized"
Stagnant and recognizable when repeated often
Dangerously "comfortable"

Ideally, learning music theory ought to open a breeding ground of melodic creation. The problem is that a student can get trapped into playing scale, scale, scale, or mode, mode, mode. Even an occasional arpeggio can be tiresome without the higher compositional principles of contrary motion or phrasing. But, it's a start, and unless you know the **guide tones** of the chord, the notes of the scale, the notes around them and the "gravitational pull," all you are capable of generating is the musical equivalent of phonetic babble.

Knowing "riffs" or "licks" is actually a good starting point and lends itself as a terrific send-off for further melodic and harmonic development. The idea is to stretch these phrases by applying principle to content-taking the pattern to the next level.

Learn as many scales and arpeggio patterns as you can. Learn them in your brain and fingers so that the notes within them can be tagged and identified at the speed of light. The next step is to take patterns you like, "steal" them from your favorite players, and "push the principle." Certainly transpose them to other keys, but why stop there? The next step is to vary them rhythmically, take notes out, add notes, throw in an altering chord, but apply sound music theory along the way.

Sound too cerebral? Many argue that music is just "created." It comes from nowhere. We would argue that the great musicians only make it *seem* like it came from nowhere. The beauty is we can never know what "analytical" processes go on in an artist's brain, all we have is the aural result. We can, however, guess and along the way come up with some unique and individual concepts of our own.

Let's take a sample pattern or riff and do some exploring. This is a nice little 'ii V7' riff in the key of F Major.

Now it's easily moved into the same song, different chord environment, but easily repeatable in rhythmic and melodic content:

Base Pattern

Base Pattern within the same key, new chords

Note we haven't left the key, and we are still able to maintain at least a resemblance to the Base Pattern. Now we are just "improvising" on the tonic chord. We've added a "freshness" simply by changing the harmonic environment.

Next we can totally transpose into a new key center by moving everything up a whole step. This is not uncommon in Western (European) music, especially in jazz.

Base Pattern transposed in a different tonal center

Let's think "rhythm" and alter the base pattern slightly with a little rhythmic embellishment:

We have changed very little melodically, and deliver a consistency in our "composition."

Rhythmic variation of Base Pattern

Simplified, emphasizing extracting chord tones

We don't necessarily have to make it more complex, we can also *simplify*. Here we remove the chaff relying on the more nutritious chord tones. You don't always have to ADD notes! (*This is where the benefit of music theory DOES have its place…*)

105

Another trick would be taking rhythmic ideas within a riff and swapping them. Melodic content stays close, and though we haven't made it any more complex, we give the impression of something new:

Swap rhythmic base of each measure

We can have just as much fun by taking one appealing rhythmic motif, and repeating it through both measures:

Extract single motif first measure only

Even more single motive extraction

And, of course, just as much fun grabbing yet another fun melodic motif. Again, it won't have to be complicated to *you*, but your audience will consider you quite clever!

Note that you don't *abandon* music theory. The underlying sound, academic principles remain; we have emphasis on the appropriate chord tones, some gentle tension/resolution motion, yet we haven't completely exhausted the endless possibilities on just two measures.

Improvisation does not have to be intimidating! It merely requires a good starting point, and the tiniest bit of creativity. Combine the two approaches, **Pattern Based and Theory Based**, and you can come up with your own beautiful solos much more quickly.

Extra Credit:

Find your favorite artists' licks, preferably short and less an octave. Transpose them into all four **FFcP** patterns. Next, transpose them into the upper frets.

Other instrumentalists will have to learn different fingerings for all 12 keys. For the mandolinist using the **FFcP** approach, only **4** fingerings are necessary. *You can learn the riffs in all 12 keys in 1/3 the time!*

Now, let's have some fun with the chord changes from "Satin Doll," but use sample melodic motiffs from "Fascinating Rhythm." Note on the next page, the harmonic analysis will help you develop the scale resources helpful to improvising on the changes…

Fascinatin' Doll

 Track #38

Ted Eschliman

107

Harmonic Analysis of Tonal Centers

This is an example of how you can pencil over your music for quick harmonic recognition:

Fascinatin' Doll

Ted Eschliman

Notes:

*Remember you can substitute an **Altered Scale** for many of the **V7** chords for stronger "motion."

*The D Major Key Centers could also be thought of as the **V of V** (V of G, or **Secondary Dominant**).

*The G Key Center descension to Gb is a 1/2 step shift. This '**ii V7**' application is quite common.

*The iii7 chord in Meas.10 is a common substitution for the I chord.

*The ♯iidim7 is a common chromatic chord move in swing.

Bonus CD tracks

 Track #39 Chick'n Apple Scrapple (Don Stiernberg, guitar and mandolin)

 Track #40 Fascinatin' Doll (Don Stiernberg, guitar and mandolin)

 Track #41 Yes, I'll Always Be There (Don Stiernberg, guitar and mandolin)

Please visit www.JazzMando.com for more accompaniment jam tracks.
www.JazzMando.com/webtracks.shtml

Special thanks to **John Eubanks** for Rhythm Guitar on many tracks, and coordinating the New Orleans "Katrina Players" rhythm section on tracks #12, #14, #32, #37, and #38.

CD Mastering by Tim Pratt, Grouchy Peanut Studio, Lincoln, Nebraska.

Part of the Team:
On Ensemble Playing

We have to face the reality of the current relevance of the role of the mandolin in the traditional jazz ensemble. Frankly, there is no deeply rooted tradition, and it's up to the current generation of players to create one!

You won't see our instrument competing even in the background rhythm section of a blazing big band. Even a prominent position in an acoustic gypsy string band is a relatively new phenomenon for mandolin, and not consistently in the perception of the general public.

All is not lost; this lack of convention allows the current generation of jazz mandolinists to "write" the rules. With a bit of out-of-the-box thinking, and a basic understanding of the elements of music: **melody, rhythm, and harmony**, we can take the best of what the mandolin has to offer, and blaze a whole new trail of significance.

Working within "monophonic" limitations

A "linear" instrument like a sax or trumpet, won't be "comping" on chords. A drummer won't be kicking off the head with a theme-setting melody. Just as these players are able to grapple with limitations and be thought of as *jazz* instruments, a mandolinist must think to take advantage of its strengths. These might include the ability to play four notes simultaneously (chords), the rhythmic treble snap and slap allows a percussive role, and of course in smaller ensembles, the bearer of melody.

Melody

Barring acoustic obstacles (larger and louder instruments), we *can* make sweet melodies. An important driving force in your playing must be the approach to phrasing; you want to think and "breathe" like a wind instrument. This means sustaining by connecting your notes as a clarinetist would. With attention to technique, you can overcome the inherent challenge by keeping your fingers close to the fretboard; bleeding one note into the next. The **FFcP** approach sets you up beautifully for this.

Rhythm

If you are/were a Bluegrass or folk musician, you are no stranger to the "chop" chord, the "back beat" role of the mandolin. This is the timekeeper in this arena, much as the hi hat cymbal is to jazz. Unlike Bluegrass where rhythmic simplicity rules, you'll want to contribute something more sophisticated. You can certainly offer a simple four-to-a-bar Gypsy "chunk" or a more complex Latin "Clave" rhythm.

How you mute with your left hand, how you accent with your right gives you a rich range of opportunity to contribute to the band's rhythm. Closing or "muting" the right fingers give you control over the degree of percussiveness of the chord.

Big caution: syncopated Funk or pyrotechnic R & B, you don't want to rhythmically conflict with the other "rhythm" players. You must support; never forsake collaboration for complexity!

Harmony: Melodic (linear)

Mimic the melody by harmonizing in parallel a **6th** or a **3rd** away. Gently introduce a few signature tremolos in a slow ballad, and you add a touch no other instrument but a mandolin can do. You can also offer a distinct counter melody by picking up where the melody phrase subsides, and getting out of the way when it intensifies. (This could almost be described as a "call and response.")

Remember you are fighting the inherent weakness of string "decay." You can't blow or bow harder after picking the note, so you must surmount that weakness with good finger control and accurate right-hand/left-hand coordination.

Harmony: Chords (horizontal)

Help define the song's harmony by playing chords, but remember you work within the confines of a soprano instrument. This is not bad; even thought you are weak on bass note production, in exchange you get to play the "color" tones of chord extension, the cool **13ths**, **♯9** chords, **or m7♭5**.... (*See the section on Chord Economics*)

A warning here is to be courteous in your coordination with other comping instruments (and the soloist). If you add a 9 to the chord, the guitar can't be conflicting with a ♯9. Err on the sparse side.

Be indispensable...

The key in ensemble participation: **Do that which no one else is doing**. Complement by adding variety, support by reinforcing. Making your contributions totally irreplaceable, your place in the band is inimitable. Strive to be unique, but take advantage of the lush license jazz mandolinists enjoy, liberated from convention or stereotype.

Parting Thoughts

FFcP

We've asked you to play the bulk of the exercises in the book with closed fingerings. Don't feel like you need to do this all the time in "real world" playing. The open strings are good; you would never get away from them, however, if you didn't develop strength and dexterity in your 3rd and 4th fingers. Hopefully by now, working through this material you've discovered the powerful by-products of finger control and a healthy sustain. (Good tone is all about what goes on between the notes-that magical intersection of the release of one note and the attack of the second.)

Now that you've mastered closed positions, go out and ADD open strings!

Chord Melody

If you started from the beginning of the book and worked your way through, you may have observed a progression, from linear or melodic to vertical, or chords. In improvising, you need an integrated understanding of both, and as you approach them in more sophisticated chord/melody playing, the intersection of these worlds will start to make more sense.

Instrument Considerations

Each of us is endowed with his/her own preferences for instrument mechanics, just as each of us differs in physical attributes. You can be stuck with short pudgy digits like the author, or wield the banana finger span of Mike Marshall. You can swing your wrists in baseball bat wielding motions like Sam Bush, or control your pick with the infinite precision and finesse of Evan Marshall. We'll register that in general, with jazz you would be better off with medium to medium light strings and a lower action. This will vary with the acoustical demands and size of ensemble, of course, but you are less likely to need the stout, banjo-killing projection of Heavy strings/High action. The closed finger approach is incentive enough to strive for an instrument that will bless you with sustain, comfort, and endurance.

Listening

There is simply no substitute for listening to music. You could never learn the nuance and subtle conventions of jazz without hearing it played first. Not to undermine the value of reading and standard notation, but the tradition of jazz is most certainly an aural one. For every hour you play, spend three listening. Don't limit yourself to mandolinists, either. Horn players can teach you phrasing, piano players and guitarists can teach you harmonic tricks, and there are always magic percussive qualities you can lift off a good drummer.

Mark your music

This has been suggested before, but especially if you're just starting out analyzing chord functions, pencil your tonal centers in your music. Find your '**ii V7 I**,' your dominant, prep, and tonic chords. Pencil in alternative turnaround progressions until you get to the point they become automatic. If nothing else, other members reading your music will be on the same page as you. (Literally…)

Not one is right.

Remember, jazz is an art, not a science. There are some basic principles and conventions, but these are far outweighed by interpretation and creative opportunity. Go with the flow, be willing to adapt to other musicians' interpretations. Vagueness begets creative license, and always remember the words of the great legend, Jethro Burns, "You're either on the right note or only one fret away from the right note!"

*The beauty of jazz is the blur
between intent and mistake.*

About the Author

Ted Eschliman *graduated from the University of Nebraska in 1980 with a Bachelor of Music in Education as a trombone major, where he also taught undergraduate music theory. A part time arranger, he discovered his love for the studio in the 90s, writing and producing three solo albums, as well as dabbling at copy-writing and freelance studio singing for a local jingle company. Despite his full-time commitments as part owner and marketing director of a Nebraska retail music store chain, Dietze Music, he continued to perform jingles and write instrumental music beds for local radio stations, as well as co-write music for area Contemporary Christian artists in his spare time.*

A self-professed "hack" multi-instrumentalist, Eschliman developed his jazz chops as keyboardist/manager of a local jazz quartet. In 1998, enchanted by the perfect symmetry and jazz potential of his first mandolin, it became a permanent passion to translate his knowledge of jazz and music theory to its fretboard. March of 2003 was premier of his popular website, jazzmando.com, a journal of these discoveries for other aspiring jazz mandolinists.

Eschliman has been a regular contributor for the popular Mel Bay online webzine, www.mandolinsessions.com., and unofficial design consultant for Rigel Mandolins, and co-moderator of the widely popular website discussion board, www.mandolincafe.com.

Acknowledgements

I Think therefore I jam

This book would not have been possible without the help and contributions of some key individuals. At the risk of leaving some important people out, I'm going to list some of them…

Scott Tichenor of the world renowned website, Mandolincafe.com, for showing me that it's possible to take something you enjoy and earnestly (and systematically!) share it with the world. The countless labor and resources he has put into this site has created a whole cyber community of mandolinists willing to share and encourage in our little eight-stringed wonder.

Don Stiernberg, world-class jazz mandolinist and all around nice guy, thanks for the support and kind words throughout the project. Don is my greatest hope for the art of jazz mandolin. Some of us can only talk about it. He can DO it…

Michael Lampert, electric jazz mandolin pioneer, always the voice of reason and common sense, thanks for listening and being willing to bounce off ideas on the practical side of jazz theory.

Joe Carr, another mentor and groundbreaking mandolin methodologist, thank you for the "streetwise" insights into the publishing industry, and giving me a "leg up" in writing columns for Mel Bay's Mandolin Sessions. Bill Bay, thanks also for believing in me enough to give me a chance at this.

The "Proofer's Club" who diligently practiced through the exercises and helped me find mistakes before the readers, Anton Darby, Steve Scott, Eric Nelson, Robert Althouse, Bill Eberhart, Jim Bryan, Andy Sicard, Dale Ludewig, Bryan Claffey, and a few others who shot positive feedback and constructive critique along the way.

A special thanks to Dion Morriss and Anton Darby for the extra efforts to help clean up the mandolinsessions.com articles, sparing me much global embarrassment. Their advice and counsel were far above the call of duty.

Peter Mix of New Millennium Acoustic Design, thanks for fueling my endless passion for innovative mandolin design, and new ways of making an instrument that "blows" like a clarinet, but comps like an L-4.

Of course it almost goes without saying, the patience and support of a good wife can take anyone exponentially farther; thanks to Robin Eschliman, my better half, for the willingness to let a few things slide around the house while completing this year long task. She and daughter Coco, (my "women") fill my life with so much joy, and are really the only thing that could possibly eclipse my passion for jazz mandolinning.

A motivation to serve, nurtured by personal faith and local church community has been the engine to see this project to its end. Art is also more powerful when fueled by spiritual meaning. For the opportunity to express music in my personal life that extends into this realm, I thank God.

Mandolin Chord User Template

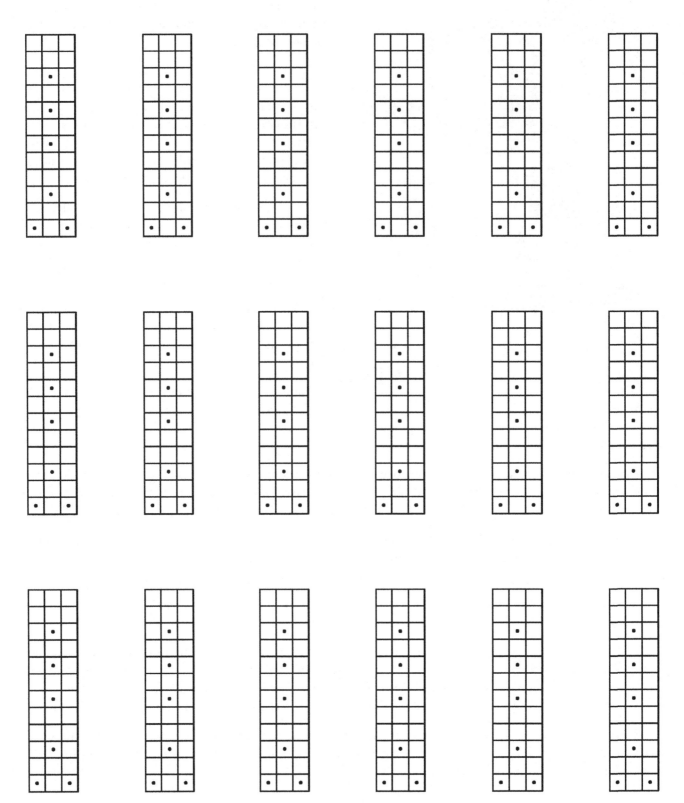

Hint: Make copies of this page for your own set of blanks.
www.jazzmando.com

Mandolin Chord User Template

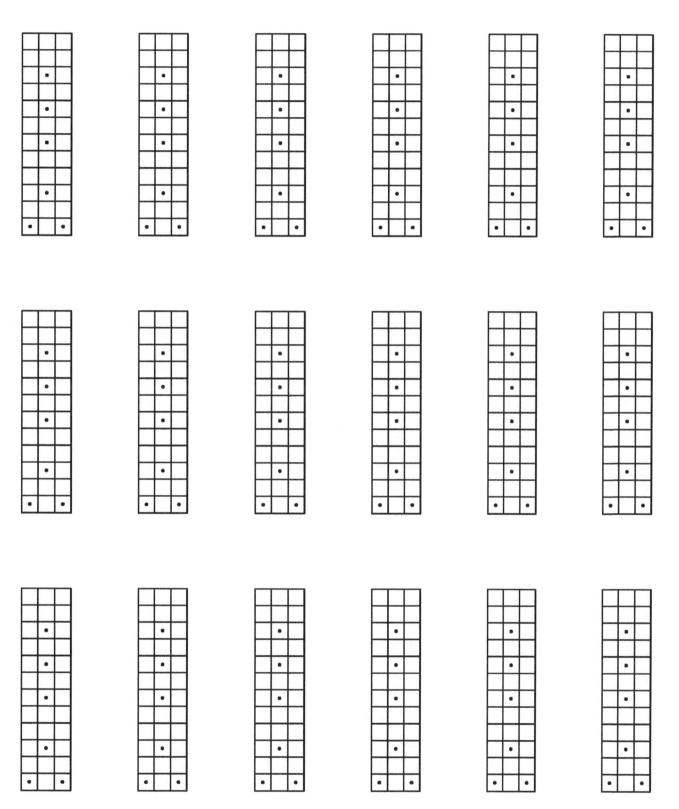

Hint: Make copies of this page for your own set of blanks.
www.jazzmando.com

Mandolin Chord User Template

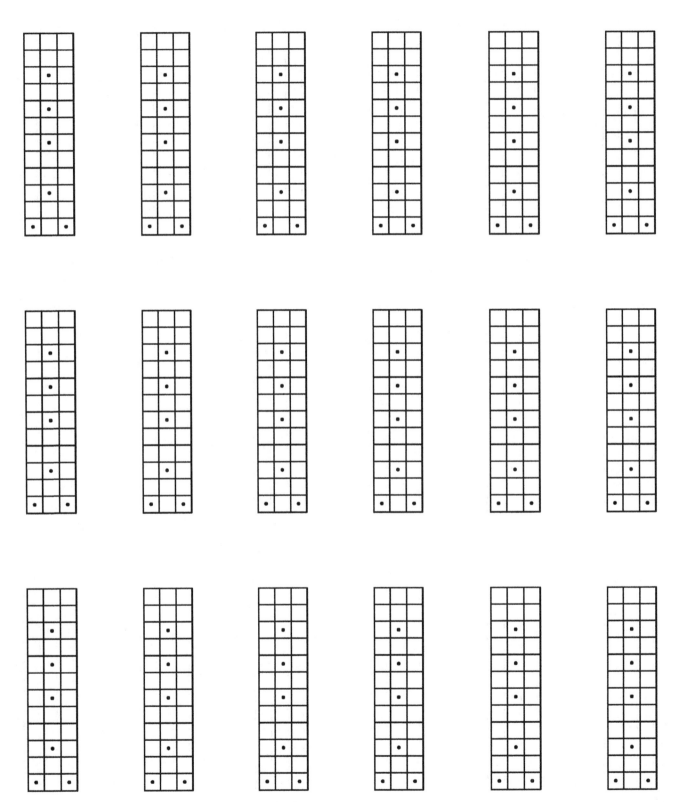

Mandolin Chord User Template

Made in the USA
Coppell, TX
02 September 2020